WHO BETTER THAN YOU?

WHO BETTER THAN YOU?

The Art of
Healthy Arrogance
& Dreaming
Big

WILL PACKER

Harmony · New York

Published in the United States by Harmony Books, an imprint of Random House, a division of Penguin Random House LLC, New York.

Harmony Books is a registered trademark, and the Circle colophon is a trademark of Penguin Random House LLC.

LIBRARY OF CONGRESS CATALOGING-IN-PUBLICATION DATA
Names: Packer, Will, author.
Title: Who better than you? / Will Packer.
Description: First edition. | New York, NY : Harmony, [2025] | Includes index.
Identifiers: LCCN 2024012630 (print) | LCCN 2024012631 (ebook) |
    ISBN 9780593582169 (hardcover) | ISBN 9780593582176 (ebook)
Subjects: LCSH: Packer, Will. | Success. | Success in business. | Motion picture producers and
    directors—United States.
Classification: LCC BJ1611.2 .P27 2025 (print) | LCC BJ1611.2 (ebook) |
    DDC 650.1—dc23/eng/20240705
LC record available at https://lccn.loc.gov/2024012630
LC ebook record available at https://lccn.loc.gov/2024012631

Printed in the United States of America on acid-free paper
HarmonyBooks.com | RandomHouseBooks.com

9 8 7 6 5 4 3 2 1

First Edition

Book design by Fritz Metsch

For Pops.
That Boy is still trying to do good. Miss you.

CONTENTS

INTRODUCTION

If You Want to Have What Others Won't, You Have to Do What Others Don't

In Defense of "Healthy Arrogance"

I hate "introductions." I hate prologues, prefaces, preambles . . . anything that stands in the way of getting to the actual good stuff. You may be the same way. I can imagine you thinking, "Will, I read your book title. I read the back cover. It was interesting enough, so I bought your stupid book. Now I'm ready to get into it. What are we waiting on?!" Prologues and introductions are like buying a ticket to a movie, sitting down in the theater, and then having to sit through a trailer . . . for *that* movie. But the editor said I just *had* to have one, so here we are. I'll try to make it as painless as possible.

"If you want to have what others won't, you have to do what others don't" is the motto of the Packer family. My wife and four kids are "The Six-Pack" on our group text. I may be a big Hollywood producer, but when my dad jokes get left on "read" by all five of my nearest and dearest, I make myself feel better by reducing their inheritances and giving their percentages to someone more deserving . . . Suki. Suki is our Portuguese water dog, and she's up to like 50 percent of the Packer family estate right now.

This concept of doing what others don't in order to reach your goals means assigning a value and priority level to what you want, then being honest about what it will take to get there. Everybody's always saying "Go for it!" when what they really mean is "Go for it . . . in a responsible and safe manner that leaves you with a traditional fallback plan in case things go wrong!" When they say "Live your dream!" they really mean "Live your dream . . . as long as it relates to your college major and comes with a 401(k) and two weeks of vacation." They mean work really hard at chasing stability.

But the only way you're ever going to be mega-successful is by taking risks. Playing it safe is like really cheap toothpaste. It may get the job done, but it leaves an aftertaste and nobody wants to kiss you. Start by dreaming big and dreaming in full rich color. Some of us have never been given permission to do this. You're told to be conservative and overcautious. Forget that. Give yourself license to dream as vivid, bright, and detailed as possible.

"No risk, no reward" is not a new concept. But what nobody talks about is how in order to take those risks, you need what I like to call "healthy arrogance."

I remember at an international screening for my movie *Ride Along,* I introduced the stars Kevin Hart and Ice Cube in the signature Will Packer way. I was hyping up that crowd with so much confidence and energy that when I walked offstage, Kevin, the forever joker, said, "Will, these people don't know who the hell you are! You always go out there and grab the mic, with 'I'm Will Packer,' like that's supposed to mean something. You ain't shit! But you act like they know who you are. They don't!"

"Yeah," I said with a smirk, "but they should. That's their fault, not mine."

I've been underestimated much of my life, for lots of different reasons, some of which are (1) I didn't come from Hollywood, (2) I'm not a wealthy white dude, and (3) I'm not six foot two. Some people never think twice about looking past me. I've always used that to my advantage.

> {Narrator: Just like in a movie, every now and then there is someone to help clarify certain things and keep the lead characters honest. That's me. I'm your narrator. I won't be around much, but every now and then Will Packer needs me to keep him honest whether he realizes it or not. For example, I'm not sure how relevant the "height underestimation" concept he's introducing is; there are plenty of really successful short people. But as you were.}

Oftentimes, we think having a great idea or possessing talent is the sole determinant of our success. However, I've learned that my unique skill set is the ability to take a great idea and sell it to others, then figure out how to bring it into the world, and finally deliver it in the most exciting way possible. I learned early on that this has a name: "producer." Producing movies and TV is a unique endeavor that combines artistic expertise, business acumen, salesmanship, relationship building, logistics, and, most important, leadership ability.

I learned this early on, well before producing $100 million–grossing movies, with my first film, which was made for (barely) $20,000, called *Chocolate City*.

My former business partner and still close friend Rob Hardy and I did what others don't by not only making that first movie when we were still juniors in college but also by celebrating the premiere to the hilt. We were so ambitious; we threw an all-out, blowout black-tie affair in the world-famous Florida A&M University Lee Hall student auditorium. And by *world-famous* I mean that kids on that campus and *only* on that campus know about it.

Here's where the healthy arrogance comes in.

In order to get into our premiere, everybody who was invited was required to get all dressed up in formalwear. That's right, we made a bunch of broke college students wear ball gowns and rent tuxedos. The vibe was a mash-up of a twelfth-grade prom and Beyoncé and Jay-Z's wedding. Okay, we didn't have seventy thousand orchids flown in from Thailand, but our guest list was almost as exclusive.

Our invitees were told they could bring only one person. We were very strict about it. Even the star of the movie, Kelsey Scott, didn't receive tickets for both of her parents. We were like, "Listen, you only get a plus-one. Who do you love more? Mom or Dad?" I still owe Kelsey an apology to this day for that Sophie's choice, but that's how brazen we were.

Plus-ones and penguin suits were not even the tip of the iceberg. I'll never forget standing onstage to introduce *Chocolate City,* our first movie ever, to the students. I looked down at the front row, which was empty. That was intentional. Rob and I had the audacity (aka healthy arrogance) to save seats for the biggest VIPs in Hollywood. We invited the chairmen of Sony, Paramount, Disney, Fox, Warner Bros., and Universal. I'd say "chairpeople" but that's just unnecessary since they were all men at the time. I'd say "white men" but that's implicit in the whole folks-who-run-Hollywood-studios thing, right? I even invited Oprah. I did not want to invite Oprah.

"Baby, you *got* to invite Oprah," my mom insisted.

"I don't know Oprah!" I cried.

"You don't know all those other people either!" she shot back.

"All right, you got a point, Ma." So, I invited Oprah. I only gave O a plus-one too. Whether she wanted to invite Stedman or Gayle didn't matter to me. But she'd have to choose.

People were kind of upset that the front row was open because the auditorium was packed like a sardine can, and it was standing-room only. Too bad. I had to be prepared. What if a fleet of private jets showed up that day in Leon County at the Tallahassee Regional Airport looking for the *Chocolate City* premiere? Then what? Exactly. I was prepared.

There's a moment from that night indelibly etched into my

memory—the reaction of the crowd, hooting and hollering every time they saw someone they knew. Repping for a particular dorm when it was shown on-screen or loudly doing sorority/fraternity calls whenever their members came on. It was a big party. These students were having a *ball.*

I was sitting next to my dad, who was never easily impressed with anything. To be honest, I don't think he was that impressed with *Chocolate City.* It wasn't a great movie if you didn't know people in it. If I'm being honest, it probably wasn't that great even if you did. But hey, it was my first movie. What do you expect? There was one particular scene in which birds were chirping so loudly in the background you couldn't even hear the dialogue. Amateur filmmaking stuff. Filmmaking lesson number 308: Pay for a sound mixer.

Having said that, I could tell that my dad was profoundly moved by the enthusiasm of the audience. Were they laughing at the amateurishness of it, especially after someone shouted, "Where are all these damn birds?!" Yes. Yes, they were. But they were also *loving* this movie. It was a big deal. They saw themselves on-screen, and that meant a lot. That didn't happen much in 1994.

Someone had made a film with them and people like them in it. It wasn't that the movie was such a great piece of art; it was the fact that it existed that felt like a win. Felt like empowerment. Felt like freedom.

Sometimes doing what others don't means dreaming bigger than everybody else. It took pure unmitigated gall to save a row for Hollywood executives. I didn't care if someone else didn't think that was important. We asked these kids to put on formal suits, tuxes, and gowns to go to the premiere of a little $20,000 movie with the hopes that Hollywood would show up. That's dreaming in vivid HD 4K—not black and white. We dreamed colossally big. We saw the details, the colors, the specificity. Some unknown faraway sky was the limit—not the ceiling, not the sun, not outer space, but a galaxy far, far away. Others would and did call us crazy.

The key to being successful is first thinking that you're just that great and carrying yourself accordingly. It's a confidence you have to exude so surely that others can't help but recognize it. That's healthy arrogance. If you act like your goals are essential, it forces everyone else to as well.

We embraced the power of naïveté. If I knew then what I know now, I wouldn't have done it. Read that last sentence again and apply it to some uncertainty you may be facing right now. Even back then I realized there was power in the unknown, so I just went for it. If I knew how hard it was to be a successful movie producer, I might've said, "You know what? This industry is crazy. I'm going to try something else." In your own journey, you don't have to know everything now.

I took myself and my dreams seriously. Still do. One of the big things I tell people when they pitch me projects is "If you don't believe in this wholeheartedly, don't even try. If I can't tell that you one thousand percent honestly and fiercely believe that it's going to work, is going to be amazing, and I'm going to regret it if I don't produce it—then why would I take a chance on it?" People could tell how passionate we were, so they believed that our movie was special and rented those tuxes. I'm not saying everybody knew I was going to be a successful film producer, but people felt like, "Will is super driven and crazy enough. He's going to be successful at something." I had that kind of energy. Still do.

No dream is too absurd. At the end of the day, what is absurdity? The dream of becoming a filmmaker itself seemed preposterous. I didn't know one person in Hollywood, not one. Didn't know a single person who had been successful in the movie business, not one. I'm living proof that your most far-fetched idea or goal is possible with a little healthy arrogance. Do what others don't.

Have no shame in your game. To other people your dream might seem ridiculous, but you have to know better. They're the ones who should be embarrassed for doubting you.

Nobody's dream is better or bigger than yours. So act accordingly.

Of course, none of the so-called VIPs showed up to the *world* premiere for *Chocolate City*. Not a single one of 'em RSVP'd, and none of their assistants even called back to acknowledge receipt of their invites. Turns out Oprah Winfrey did not have to choose between Stedman and Gayle because Oprah Winfrey *did not come.* And while that front row may have been completely empty, every other seat in the auditorium was taken. That's when I had a record-scratching life epiphany.

I wasn't going to be making my movies for the "important" people in the front row who couldn't be bothered to show up. I was making them for everybody else. You know, the *actually* important people. The standing-room-only folks who spent their hard-earned money to rent formalwear for a student film. I made it for Kelsey Scott's lovely parent—just the one parent though, not the other one. Oftentimes we're living our lives for the people that don't really matter. That small percentage of people that are the front-row folks, we think we need their validation and affirmation. We should be living our lives and doing our best work for everybody else who will receive it, appreciate it, and cheer it on.

You don't have to be an aspiring filmmaker to read this book, but maybe my success as a Hollywood producer brought you here. My area of expertise is storytelling. And as a storyteller, I have had the privilege of crafting narratives that have entertained audiences around the world. This is not exactly a book about making movies. It's not quite a memoir. It's a deeply personal account of the lessons I've learned on my journey to the level I've reached today. Some would say that's the top. Some wouldn't. Neither matter, and in this book I'll tell you why.

The entertainment industry has a way of throwing unexpected curveballs, and it is in those moments of chaos and confusion that painful instruction can occur, some of the funniest stories are born, and many of the greatest lessons are learned. From on-set mishaps to the quirks and idiosyncrasies of the talented individuals I have collaborated with, I hope these hard-earned lessons will make you laugh and smile while opening your eyes and ears to new ways of thinking and, more important, doing.

One of the most important things this book will explore is the manner by which a person controls their own life: the concept of self-determination. Too often we're waiting for someone else to hand us the keys that open the doors to our goals. And we want that person to not just give us the keys but also show us how to use them. You will already be closer to obtaining your personal level of greatness when you understand that *you* are the key. *You* are the secret sauce. *You* are the person you've been waiting on to give you the leg up that will make all the difference. Who better than you? By realizing that you already have access to that power, you are closer to unlocking it. Closer to producing a blockbuster life, embarking on an extraordinary career path, or maybe just having the audacity to put on your own blowout affair celebrating who else? You! Just remember one thing, and this much I know to be true . . . Oprah ain't coming.

WHO BETTER THAN YOU?

1

You Gon' Die Tonight!

Expecting the Unexpected Is Essential

Success is a bottom-line business. You are either producing or you're not. My *job* is to produce. But even if you don't work in the movie industry, if you want to reach the top of your game you will have to make things happen. That means solving all types of problems. Of course, problem-solving is less about finding ways to overcome adversity than it is about dealing with the variables that life constantly throws at you. Knowing what's coming and being prepared to deal with it is one thing. But it's the unknown that truly tests your resolve. Fair or not, you'll be judged by how you handle uncertainty.

Kevin Hart is my very good friend. In many ways our career trajectories parallel each other. Since connecting, we've found a way to work together at almost every stage of our professional lives. Kevin is a lovely, giving human who is loyal to a fault to those closest to him. Kevin is also a diabolical rascal spawn of Satan who almost ended my career just as it was starting to really take off.

I first worked with him on *Think Like a Man,* which opened number one at the box office and signaled to Hollywood that Kevin Hart was ready to break out. *Ride Along* was our next film together and the stakes were high. Where *Think Like a Man* was an ensemble comedy, *Ride Along* was a clear two-hander with Kev being the sole comedic driver opposite OG legend and consummate straight man Ice Cube. This was a chance to show that *Think Like a Man* wasn't a fluke and that Kevin really was a box-office draw. Also the *Ride Along* budget was more than twice that of *Think Like a Man,* so of course that brought added pressure. This movie was a big deal and a huge opportunity. All eyes were on us—both of us—to see if we could deliver at this level.

We were a couple weeks into shooting and things were going well. Kev and Cube had amazing chemistry, and the early scenes we shot were hilarious. Kev called me to his trailer one day at wrap and casually informed me that he had an upcoming show to do out of town the following Friday night.

"Well, we shoot next Friday, Kev," I said simply.

"I know. That's why I'm telling you now. I just need to wrap early so I can make the show."

I sighed that irritated sigh you give when one of your kids asks, "How much did that vase cost that used to sit on the shelf in the living room?"

I quickly pulled out the schedule so I could see what it would take to wrap early. That's when I realized the following Friday was the absolute worst day for Kev to have a show. Not because of what we were shooting Friday but because we had a rare Saturday shoot the next day. And not just any scene but a crucial scene in the movie where his character gets tricked by Ice Cube, which leads to a reveal of Cube's character's intentions that the whole plot centered on. Also, as fate would have it, we were shooting at a unique location in a big Atlanta marketplace that was very difficult to secure and was only available on this one particular

Saturday. It had been a nightmare to get the location, and we had spent a significant portion of our budget on site fees, production design, and so on to make it happen. We had to shoot that scene. On that day. At that location. Caught up in the throes of production, I had forgotten that scene was the following Saturday, but something told me Kev had not. I looked up from the schedule and stared at him.

"Dude, you know we shoot next Saturday."

"Do we?" *Genuine dismay.*

"Bruh, for such a good actor you're a bad actor."

"Okay, maybe I saw that Saturday shoot, but it's fine. I'll fly out Friday and come right back after the show."

"Dude. You are killing me." *Pure exasperation.* "That's way too risky. This is a big scene. Too many things can go wrong. You gotta reschedule the show."

Kevin Hart replied with two words: "I can't."

The tone of his voice was a mix of gravely serious and apologetic. It told me this was non-negotiable for some reason. This was going to be a problem. Now, to be fair, I am pretty good at solving problems. It's kind of my job. So, when I did the mental calculation I figured that, while less than ideal, he could fly down to wherever his little laugh-laugh gig was happening, sleep on the plane, and be ready for work the following day. I was more annoyed by the fact that Kev didn't mention this to me sooner. Because I'm his go-to guy who always manages to figure things out, he waited until a week before to spring this on me so I would have no choice but to work it out. He could see the frustration on my face.

"Look, Pack, you know I don't ask you for much . . ."

Pause. Whenever somebody says they don't ask for much, they are lying. That's the hallmark of somebody that asks for shit *all the time.* Kev is no exception.

". . . but, this is the biggest show of my life. I'm taping my new comedy special next Friday night at Madison Square Garden!"

{Narrator: So you know the scene in a movie where everything freezes and time stands still? Well, that's what happened next, except the only thing that stood still was Will. Will froze in that moment.}

"Did you hear what I said?" Kev asked.

"You're filming a comedy special? In New York?! In between *two* of our shooting days?! On the biggest movie of our careers?! And you're just now telling me?!" I exploded.

"You know I don't ask you for much," he repeated.

It took everything I had not to jump on this man and choke him in his own trailer.

Before we continue, I would like to explain that for the most part I resist using foul language and expletives in this book. However, it would be impossible for you to understand the internal dynamics of my relationship with Mr. Hart if I didn't make it clear that on that day I dropped enough bleeps and bombs to make Samuel L. Jackson proud.

"Pack, it'll be fine. If you can just figure out how to wrap a little early on Friday, then we'll take a jet and fly to New York that night, then turn right around, and be back on set the next morning."

We? Did he just say *we*?

He continued, "This is a big night for me. I want you and Tim to be there. I've got room on the jet. You can even bring the wives. Plus, that way you'll be there so you can see to it yourself that everything goes according to plan."

This guy is good. He knew by offering to fly director Tim Story and me up with him I would feel more comfortable. He knew I'd take solace in the fact that I would be there to personally ensure he got back on time. And he even threw in that we could bring our wives. I told you, he's good. So is the devil.

The fateful Friday arrived, and we wrapped filming early according to plan. Tim and I jumped on the jet with Kev and our wives, Heather and Vicky. Everyone was in a great mood. Excited to see our guy rock MSG on his big night. Kev did not disappoint.

We landed in New York without event, and the show was fantastic. His performance was spectacular, and everyone was there. All the New York celebs—from Jay-Z to Seinfeld and Dave Chappelle to J.Lo—showed up for Kev. And they loved it. We had great seats in the second row, and it was incredible to watch a master perform at the top of his game in the same venue where Mike put up a double nickel, Ali defeated Frazier, and Jadakiss destroyed the entire Dipset posse with one freestyle. True Kevin Hart fans will realize this was his *Let Me Explain* stand-up special, and if you look carefully you can see my wife Heather and me baring all our teeth as we fall out laughing in the audience.

When the show ended, we all went backstage where Kev received a hero's welcome from all his celebrity friends. The greenroom was packed with well-wishers giving pats on the back and taking selfies and shots with the man of the hour. I didn't love that he was drinking, but it wasn't excessive and this was his moment so I didn't say anything. After a little bit I turned to Tim and said, "All right, we should start getting ready to head out." He nodded in agreement. We were a large group, so I knew it would take a second to wrangle everyone. As I started going around the room saying "Let's get ready to roll, guys," a young lady came up to me and asked, "Are you guys going to the afterparty now?"

Ummm, excuse me? Another one of Kev's crew overheard her and said, "Yep, we're headed over right now!"

This *was not* part of the plan. I had done all the permutations for how the night needed to go in order to make it back on time and knew we needed to get off the ground by 3:17 A.M. at the *absolute* latest, which meant we needed to leave for Teterboro by 2:38 A.M. If we were even five minutes late, not only would we lose our return flight window, we'd be forced to find new pilots. An afterparty put that plan in serious jeopardy.

I immediately started looking around for Kev. I found him in the corner talking to Jay-Z. I walked right up to them. "Excuse me, Jay. Mr. Z. Sorry to interrupt. Just need Kevin for a quick second. By the way, *Blueprint 2* is a criminally underrated album." I couldn't tell if Jay-Z was amused or not. *{Narrator: Jay-Z was not amused.}*

I pulled Kev to the side.

"What afterparty?! You didn't say anything about an after-party!"

He gave me the "I could've sworn I mentioned that" face.

"It's some stupid thing they committed me to. I just gotta show up for a second. It's contractual." He said it like it was the most awful thing but he'd just have to tough it out. I didn't have time to unpack who this "they" was that was not named Kevin Hart or Will Packer and didn't have millions of dollars on the line if "we" didn't show up back in Atlanta on time the next morning.

"All right, then we gotta go to the party now!" I said and immediately turned into the backstage grinch. I started going around and taking drinks and food plates out of people's hands. "Sorry, time to wrap it up! Gotta go, guys! Last selfie! You don't have to go home, but . . ." It was like herding cats, but all the celebs started scrambling to get ready to leave because it was clear that I was an important person of authority and they needed to listen to me.

{Narrator: That is not true at all. No one cared. Will was largely ignored as he stood in the middle of the greenroom yelling that it was time to go. It wasn't until Kevin Hart said "Okay, let's roll, y'all" that people started moving.}

I figured that even with this afterparty curveball, if we actually went to the venue and just did a walk-through we could still make our window. Of course, my calculations were dependent on one component that all people of African descent must know prior to any party or group outing: *Who all gon' be there?*

Apparently, everyone was going to be there because all the celebrities and stars were packing up to head over with us. Our already unwieldy group was now a gargantuan slow-moving mix of high-profile actors, athletes, and entertainers heading to an NYC nightclub. My stomach started to turn as I checked the time. We had about an hour to get in and get out. As we stepped into the club, the crowd started chanting "KE-VIN! KE-VIN!" We were ushered into a VIP section like a huge swarm of locusts. Kev plopped down, clearly drained but still buzzing from how good the show went. "Don't get too comfortable!" I yelled over the music.

"I got you, Pack. Just one drink and we're out!"

Here is another keen insight into urban culture: Your basketball team runs the city. If you live in a place where there is a professional basketball team, they own the metropolitan area. They are the reason ladies come to clubs and why each generation of non-athletes purchases increasingly larger car rims. Football teams have bigger fan bases, but football players are interchangeable to most people. They wear helmets, so they aren't as recognizable. Baseball players make more money, but no one watches baseball except men who grew up with grandfathers who owned transistor radios and people who wear Skechers. Basketball is for the *people.*

So, we're at Kevin's afterparty exactly fifty-six minutes before mandatory liftoff when I noticed the average height in the VIP section was steadily increasing, and the karat-to-gold ratio among the jewelry wearers was nearly one to one. I silently began hoping that the Knicks had a road game and that we were being approached by bejeweled butchers. Maybe it's just me, but, in my experience, butchers, chimney sweeps, and stand-up bass players tend to be sneaky tall. The only thing that gave me comfort was the fact that I didn't really know any of the players in our section. They were the guys who could afford to buy the bar, but they still had to show ID at the door. These weren't all-stars with no-trade clauses in their contracts. They were nonessential Knicks. Knick-knacks, if you will.

Only forty-seven minutes left on the clock. Ticktock, Clarice.

Just then I saw the waitress's eyes light up like a Spades player with both jokers. Because I make movies for a living, you may assume that I am employing hyperbole, but trust me, I am not. All of a sudden, the music stopped. The lights got about thirteen lumens brighter. The crowd noise died down as if everyone was a child and grown folks were talking, and people stood as if they were expecting the choir to march in. I could see the DJ lean in to the microphone like he was preparing to announce that the president had just signed an executive order mandating reparations. As I bowed my head in reverence or expectation, he screamed, "OH, SH**! Carmelo Anthony is in the building!"

As the sea of human flight delays parted, Melo marched in surrounded by a parade of waitresses carrying bottles of champagne sizzling with sparklers so bright they looked like acetylene welding torches. Carmelo walked straight up to Kevin as the waitresses began handing out bottles. There were so many that each person in the section got their own individual bottle. I tried to yell over the commotion, "I'm sure we don't need all these bottles! This feels excessive, guys! We're about to leave, but thanks anyway, really nice gesture!" The waitresses ignored me.

Melo congratulated Kev on selling out Madison Square Garden and gave him an embrace that engulfed Kev's entire body. As Carmelo's enormous arms released their captive comedian, he screamed, "You gon' die tonight! Let's turn up!" As he said that, the DJ dropped a certified club banger and everybody went absolutely bananas.

In a split second, I envisioned my entire movie and career going down the drain. I ran over to Kev in desperation. This man looked me right in my eyes and said, "Welp, *we* tried."

{Narrator: It was right then that Will knew he had effed up.}

In that moment, the pure evil genius of Kevin Hart started to sink in. He knew there was almost no possible way he could perform in the biggest arena in show business, host an afterparty, invite all his celeb friends, and still make it to Atlanta the next morning. As the star of the movie, him missing one day would imperil the budget and the production schedule and rearrange the schedule of the entire cast and crew. The studio would be furious, and it would be all his fault.

Unless, of course, the movie's producer was with him the entire time. This was Kevin Hart's plan all along.

My eyes got as wide as the Hudson River. As I looked at Kev in disbelief, the score from *The Usual Suspects* started to play and I began having flashbacks. I flashed to Kev casually mentioning his comedy show the first time. I flashed to him saying "we" would fly up to the show together. I flashed to Heather and me laughing it up *on camera* at Madison Square Garden.

I looked at my friend Kevin Hart. He was grinning from ear to ear and reaching for a champagne bottle. He looked like the devil, if Lucifer was short and Black. I went into panic mode. Melo had a vice grip on Kev's shoulder with one hand and was pouring huge shots of high-end tequila with the other.

I'd met Melo once before on the set of *Think Like a Man* when he came to visit his then wife, La La Anthony, who was one of the stars. I started trying to get his attention, desperately saying, "No, no, no! We can't do this! Kevin can't die tonight! We have to leave! We have forty minutes to get to Teterboro! Remember me? I produced the movie with La La!"

Carmelo Anthony is six foot seven. I am . . . well, I'm not. I must have looked crazy as I was literally jumping up and down trying to talk to him in the middle of the nightclub. I imagine he heard every other word. "No! Can't die! Teterboro! Remember! La La!"

He turned to Kevin as if to say "Who is this guy?"

I couldn't hear what Kevin said, but to Kev's credit, he must have given me a glowing review because Melo grabbed me with those supersized hands, and all I could think was "I wonder where he buys gloves?"

"We gon' die!" he exclaimed giddily as he signaled to a waitress to hand me a bottle.

I began to realize that I was now part of the "we" in King Melo's declaration of who would perish tonight. Now I'm trying to barter with the Emperor of Knickerbocker Kingdom for a die-tonight rain check. "How about three weeks from now, after you play the Lakers? I'd be willing to die on that night. I could actually die in the first week in June. We'd have already wrapped the film, and, let's face it, you're not getting past the first round of the playoffs, which makes it a perfect time for mutual death. Shall I send a Google Calendar invite? How about it, Melo?"

I was literally trying to figure out if I could physically carry Kevin out of the club when Carmelo must've seen the pure desperation on my face. He turned to Kev and me and said, "I'mma let y'all off this time, but next time you come to New York, it's going down. Get outta here."

Thank you, Jesus.

I grabbed the bottle of champagne out of Kev's hands, had his security clear a path toward our fleet of SUVs, and negotiated a police escort to the airport from the cops that were outside of the club. We were spinning corners on two wheels as the police sirens blared. We made the flight with three minutes to spare.

In whatever life path you choose, there will always be uncharted waters and unforeseen obstacles that arise along your way. The true test lies in your ability to adapt and adjust. I found myself in a no-win situation, and I had to figure out how to get out of it. You may never be in a nightclub with Carmelo Anthony celebrating your mutual destruction on a particular evening. But you may find yourself in a position where you have no idea how you're going to get out of it despite all your best-laid plans. As the royal poet-philosopher-flutist André the 3000th once wrote, "You can plan a pretty picnic, but you can't predict the weather."

A crisis was averted that night in NYC. Thank God Melo relented, but make no mistake, it was not an option to not get Kevin Hart back to set. If I had to walk him back to Atlanta from New York on my back, I was going to do it. I was going to be late, but I was going to at least show the studio, "Hey, I tried everything possible to get him back." I was never going to accept defeat.

If I had to identify my biggest mistake, it was forgetting to expect the unexpected that night. You must expect the unforeseen. Operating at the highest levels means while others are marveling at the thought of what could go right, you're allotting a portion of your mental capacity to staying homed in on the worst-case scenario. Doing this consistently trains your brain to think in terms of opportunities for success *and* unforeseen challenges.

Once we were in the air heading back to Atlanta, Kev looked over at me and said with a huge smile, "What a great night, huh?!" I proceeded to choke him to death right there on the plane.

> {Narrator: No he didn't. They all slept for a couple hours, landed in Atlanta, showered, and went straight to set the following morning. The scene got done, the movie got completed, and no one ever knew how close they came to disaster. Until now.}

2

Finish the Damn Deal!

Be Extraordinary from Beginning to Satisfying End

Football fans know the name Leon Lett. He is a 290-pound former defensive tackle for the Dallas Cowboys. He has quite the résumé. He was elected to the Pro Bowl twice and won three Super Bowls. But that is not what he is known for. During Super Bowl XXVII in 1993, he recovered a fumble and ran sixty-plus yards toward the end zone. The crowd went crazy. This would have been an incredible play for anyone to make, but an almost-300-pound man moving that far and that fast was a sight to behold. That big brother was flying, well, more like lumbering, but still . . . 300 pounds. You could see the moment of pure jubilation on his face as he looked up and saw himself on the jumbotron, realizing he was about to go into the NFL history books for this one play.

He ended up in the history books, all right. As Leon was gliding into certain big-man glory, a scrappy 185-pound wide receiver for the Buffalo Bills named Don Beebe was not giving up on the play. Don ran as fast as he could, but it was clear Leon had too much of a head start. He wasn't going to catch him. Lumbering Leon was going to score a touchdown. Around the ten-yard line, their fates intertwined. Leon slowed up to showboat for the crowd. It looked like he was trying to do some kind of weird arm-extended high-step dance into the end zone for the cameras. You can tell he thought he was gonna be dancing alllll night. This move gave Don just the opportunity he needed. Right before Leon crossed into the end zone, Don stripped the ball. The look on Leon's face, in that moment, is pure comedy. He looks like this is the most absurd thing possible in the entire history of absurd things. His face says, "What in the entire hell is happening right now?" It's like he was minding his business in the frozen foods section and all of a sudden some random football player comes out of nowhere and steals a lamb shank from his shopping cart. If incredulity had a mascot, it would be Leon Lett's face in that moment.

There would be no touchdown. There would be no big-man glory. Only infamy. If Leon *had* scored, I don't know if people would still be talking about it today. But I know people definitely still talk about him *not* scoring. He has become a cautionary verb for any athlete who doesn't see a play all the way through. "Oh man, that guy almost Leon Letted!" You don't want to be a Leon Lett.

To do extraordinary things you have to have an extraordinary process. Not an extraordinary start, not an extraordinary middle, but extraordinary from beginning to end. No one will remember that you started strong if you don't finish the same way. A big mistake people make is thinking they've done enough. Thinking, "I worked hard, I checked the boxes, I've done all I can." No. No, you haven't. In relationships, parenting, career, et cetera, embrace a mentality of always going above and beyond. One of my personal sayings is "Overambition is a myth of the complacent." And to me complacency is akin to death.

The saying "It's not over until it's over" applies across the board. And thank God it does because it means that even if you *don't* start strong there's still an opportunity to make up lost ground. You can be a Don Beebe.

I, like a lot of people, used to hate Tom Brady. I mean not *hate* hate him. I never met the man. But I mean, c'mon, what was there *not* to hate. He was too good-looking, his wife was too beautiful, and he won too damn much. Like *all* the time. *Nobody* likes that guy. Well, unless he's on your team. But since he could only play for one team at a time, that meant that the majority of football fans shared my disdain for Mr. I Win All the Super Bowls. Never mind that he worked his ass off year-round to reach the heights that no one else had achieved. Never mind that he was willing to put his body, mind, and spirit through an insane regimen of rigidness and discipline to sustain his level of play. I saw those as irrelevant details, and since he didn't play for my team *I didn't care.*

I especially hated Tom Brady on the eve of Super Bowl LI when his New England Patriots were taking on my adopted hometown's Atlanta Falcons. Now, to understand what was at stake you have to understand all the subtext around this game. The Falcons play in Atlanta, a vibrant southern African American–led city that many have appropriately termed a Black mecca. The Patriots represent the city of Boston, a historically white northeastern metro with a checkered history of racial relations. And by *checkered* I mean that there are parts of Boston that have been downright racist for, like, forever years. This was also February 2017. One of the most polarizing, controversial, and (to many) shocking presidential elections had just taken place a couple months prior. In elections there is always a lot of voting that takes place along racial lines, but that particular election took it to new heights. Many Black people felt like Trump was a racist, and him winning the election was further proof that the country was too. I'm not saying all Black voters voted against Trump (because they didn't), but let's just say he didn't stand a snowball's chance in hell in Atlanta.

Tom Brady, sandy-blond phenom QB for the Patriots, had

done an interview earlier that season with a Make America Great Again hat prominently placed in his locker. It was clear who he was supporting. So the stage was set. Falcons versus Patriots, Atlanta versus Boston, Black versus white, good versus evil. Okay, okay, I'm having some fun with all that; relax, I'm a storyteller! But the fact is there was definitely some palpable subtext going into this game, and for Black Falcons fans this was finally a chance to have *something* go our way. It had been a rough few months. Couple that with the fact that the Super Bowl was in Houston, another Black-led city with a vibrant African American community, and it was all the more reason for Atlanta to show up and show out for our team.

My wife and I traveled to Houston for the game, joining the sea of Atlanta supporters who flooded the city. And let me tell you, there's nothing quite like a city united behind their winning team. Atlanta was on fire, and hundreds of thousands of Atlantans and folks who look like Atlantans brought that electric energy to Houston Super Bowl weekend. It was a beautiful sight to see. The weekend was an extravaganza of celebrations. Heather and I hit it all. We attended pre-parties and concerts, afterparties and tailgates, fashion shows, cookouts, you name it. And all that is *leading up* to the game.

Now, as for the actual game, well, that was less important going in. As great a year as the team had had, the Falcons were underdogs, which was understandable with Mr. Tom *insert retch sound here* Brady on the other side. That didn't dampen Falcons fans' enthusiasm though, because, while Tommy B was in the big game seemingly every other year, it had been *eighteen years* since the Falcons sniffed it. *Eighteen years.* If you were born the year the Falcons last went to the Super Bowl, you were now old enough to vote for Donald Trump!

On Super Bowl Sunday, Heather and I got to the game early and attended a pre-kickoff VIP concert where all the top Atlanta hip-hop artists performed: Ludacris, Jeezy, 2 Chainz, Outkast, and on and on. We had a blast. Now it was game time. Our seats were directly behind the Patriots' bench, which meant we were surrounded by Patriots fans. We stood out. Not just because we were the only people for like ten rows with Falcons gear on but also because we were literally the only Black people in our entire section. True story. I settled in, mentally prepared myself for a bunch of Bostonian trash talk, and secretly prayed, "Please, chocolate baby Jesus. Don't let us get blown out and I have to hear from this mayonnaise mafia the whole game."

But then, something strange happened. The Atlanta Falcons started winning. And winning *big*. They were crushing the Patriots up and down the field! And in our section, it was *really* quiet. Well, I should say it *would* have been quiet if Heather and I hadn't been there. Now, there are fans who, when their team is winning, are gracious and respectful to the folks whose team isn't. Heather and Will Packer are not those fans. One of the reasons Heather and I get along so well is that we are wildly competitive and grade-A, premium-level trash-talkers. Doesn't matter who it is or where we are. She's from Memphis and I'm from Florida . . . trash will be talked. When we weren't cheering for the Falcons, she rooted for the Cowboys and I rode with the Tampa Bay Bucs. When our teams played we gave it to *each other . . . mercilessly.* So that just lets you know when the Falcons were upsetting the Patriots in the *Super Bowl,* by a wide margin, those Patriots fans around us didn't stand a chance. We were fist-bumping, high-fiving, and doing choreographed dances after every big play. At some point we started doing call-and-response chants to no one but ourselves:

HEATHER: Where you from?!
WILL: A-T-L!
WILL: Peace up!
HEATHER: A-Town down!

"Aren't you tired of dancing?" somebody sneered.
"Nope!" I said. "We're gonna be dancing *allllll night!*"

We had to be the most obnoxious Black people those Patriots fans had ever seen. And if we weren't, it wasn't for lack of trying. All eyes were on us, and we loved every minute of it.

Before we knew it, it was halfway through the third quarter and we were winning 28–3! That's when we started my favorite chant of the night. You know the ubiquitous sports chant that's literally any four syllables and then five claps in succession? It works with anything, like "Let's go, Fal-cons!" *Clap clap clap-clap-clap.* Well, at that point we were so far ahead we turned that chant into "Where is To-om?!" *Clap clap clap-clap-clap.* We were having a *ball*.

Around then I got a text from someone who worked in the mayor's office. They were already planning the Super Bowl parade for the following Tuesday. They wanted to have as many Atlanta celebs in it as possible and wanted to know if I was available. OF COURSE! I replied. I hit Shayla Cowan, my assistant at the time, to change my flight so I could make the Atlanta Falcons victory parade. For the game I was currently at. That was still. Being. Played. You ever see an entire *city* Leon Lett before? *In my Usher voice* Watch this.

Somewhere between the Falcons' big plays, the Packers' taunts, and the mayoral preparations, somebody forgot that this was Tom freaking Brady we were counting out. And that's when Tom Brady turned into Don Beebe.

Slowly but surely, Tom Brady did what Tom Brady does. He scored one touchdown, then a field goal, then another touchdown, while the Patriots held the Falcons scoreless. The energy in our section began to shift. My wife and I sat uncomfortably quiet, a stark contrast from the first three quarters. Patriots fans started looking around for us. Sadly for us, we weren't hard to find.

"How you doing over there, Atlanta?!" someone shouted.

"You nervous yet?" somebody else yelled.

With six minutes left in the fourth quarter, the Patriots were within eight. The Patriots fans were in a full-blown frenzy. The loud chocolate power couple didn't have a thing to cheer about. There were no dances, no fist bumps, and no chants. It was the mayonnaise mafia's time to shine! When Tom threw the game-tying two-point conversion with fifty-seven seconds on the clock, they exploded.

"There is To-om!" *Clap clap clap-clap-clap,* they chanted in unison. They were so on beat it was like they had practiced it. I hadn't seen white people that coordinated since *High School Musical.* Heather and I looked at each other in disbelief, as if to say, "Who in the *hell* stole our lamb shank?"

It was at this moment, with the game tied and heading into overtime, that I saw something that absolutely crushed my spirit.

I had always assumed that at the end of a championship game when the MVP is talking about going to Disneyland and the confetti is raining down on the players' heads, that said confetti was somehow placed in the ceiling and rigged to fall at the end of the game. But because our seats were so close to the sidelines, I could see that there were huge confetti cannons posted around the field. The reason I even noticed this is because I saw sideline staff taking the distinctive red-and-black confetti of the Falcons out of the cannons. "They probably shouldn't have loaded them prematurely anyway," I thought. But then instead of letting the cannons sit empty, they swiftly replaced the confetti. With the red, white, and blue of the Patriots! The symbolism of that simple act hit me like a ton of bricks. I nudged Heather. "But the game isn't even over yet!" she proclaimed indignantly.

"It probably is, honey. It probably is," I sighed.

You know how this story ends. With Tom "Terrific" Brady completing the greatest comeback in Super Bowl history. With Heather and I having a looooong walk out of the stadium through a sea of (probably well-earned) Bostonian vitriol. With the prideful, swagalicious city of Atlanta lumbering toward its first Super Bowl win getting stripped by scrappy Tom "Don Beebe" Brady.

{*Narrator: I'm pretty sure this is the only time in history that those two names have been interposed like that.*}

It's an absolute must to keep your eye on the finish line—whether you're a football player, a filmmaker, or strive to be any kind of achiever, frankly. I've had movie productions that were complete disasters behind the scenes before they were finished. I've had moments where everything that can go wrong does right before a movie premiere. I've run out of gas on my way to huge presentations. Had printers break down in the middle of printing scripts needed on set at that exact moment. But I never admit failure until I have to. Nobody watching my movies knows or cares what happened before they got there. The same is true in the professional business world. If you're working on something and it feels like it's going bad, if it ain't over . . . it ain't over. You can salvage it. You can salvage a victory from the jaws of defeat. Always keep working on the project, the proposal, the presentation. Because at the end of the day, all people will remember is the end result. That's what you should judge yourself by—how you finish. Get in the end zone . . . then you, your boo, and your lamb shank can dance allllll night.

TOM BRADY IS THE GREATEST!

The power of perspective is an extraordinary tool, capable of shaping our beliefs, decisions, and actions in profound ways. In March 2020 we were at the onset of the global Covid pandemic. The world was on lockdown, and I was on a Zoom call conducting a business meeting. The whole video conference as a daily way of life was a new thing in Hollywood and we were all still figuring it out. I'm sure I was unintentionally on mute. All of a sudden my phone exploded. It was like everybody I knew started texting me at once. "Oh God, what now?!" I thought, fearing something tragic related to this pandemic had occurred. I looked at my phone. Tom Brady?! WTF??? was one message. BRRRAAADDDYYYY!!!! went another. OMG. "Tom Brady died of Covid," I thought. That's the only thing that made sense. Sad, but at least now somebody else can win the Super Bowl. Then another message said, The BUCS got Brady! Wait a minute, what? I logged off the conference (my camera was accidentally pointed at the ceiling anyway) and turned on ESPN. It was true. A man I had been rooting against for years was suddenly on the Tampa Bay Bucs?! Tampa got the GOAT?

One thing about Tom Brady: You may not like him *[Narrator: Who is "you"? Just say Will. Will didn't like him]*, but you have to respect him. For his work ethic, his dedication, his passion. He truly is the embodiment of greatness. And that's the thing about being great—not everyone is going to cheer you on. Doesn't matter. You just have to keep on being great, and ask, "Who better than me?!" Just like Tom.

I didn't miss a game that Covid-stricken season. As soon as they let fans in the stadium, I was right there. Cheering on the Bucs, cheering on Tom. That year he took the Bucs to the Super Bowl. It was the first time in Super Bowl history that a team played in their home stadium. Because of Covid they only allowed twenty-five thousand actual people into the stands; they filled the rest of the stadium with cardboard cutouts of fans. You *know* who two of the real people were. Heather and I cheered, chanted, and danced the Bucs to victory in between fake cardboard fans.

"How 'bout that Tom Brady?" Heather said to me.

"What's not to *love*?!" I responded.

By the way . . . we were *still* the only Black people in our section.

3

You Ain't That Great, but You Could Be

Pushing Beyond Good

My mom was easily the first person to inspire me to greatness. I remember one time in elementary school I was really proud of myself for making the honor roll for the first time. I got all A's and B's, and when the teacher called out the "smart" kids' names, everyone applauded. That felt amazing. Then they called out the dean's list names, the straight-A kids, and I didn't really notice or care because I was still doing my grand-marshal-of-the-parade wave to fourth graders who had long since stopped clapping.

I came home, freshly minted as the new honor roll kid from Maximo Elementary School in St. Petersburg, Florida, all pumped to tell my parents about my historic achievement. I placed my honor roll certificate and report card strategically on the corner of the kitchen counter so they couldn't be missed, opened the fridge, and pretended to be pulling out the orange juice, all smug and satisfied with myself. I waited for what seemed like forever to be noticed.

My mom finally walked by, right past me, right past my

report card, and into the living room to go watch television. "Hey, baby," she said. "Close that door!"

Because, you may know, when you have a Black mama, in the South no less, you *do not* allow the cold air to be let out of the refrigerator. The level of cold air in the refrigerator determines everything. The mortgage, the light bill, the cable. You let the air out of the refrigerator, your circumstances go into the dumpster immediately. I was risking ruining our lives with that open refrigerator door. And she didn't even notice my grades.

This was not the script I had in my head.

"Yes, ma'am." I closed the door. As she started to turn back to the TV, she spotted the paper on the counter.

"What's this?"

I turned around dramatically like an understudy getting his shot on Broadway after the lead gets food poisoning. "What's whaaaat?" I exclaimed as I grinned from ear to ear. Such a bad actor. My mom walked back over to the counter, picked up my report card, perused it, and set it back down.

"Oh my goodness, that's really great," she said. "I'm so proud of you! Way to go, baby!" She kissed me on the forehead.

"Thanks, Ma," I beamed. My nine-year-old chest could not be pumped out farther. "We're going to put this on the refrigerator. Does your father know?" My dad, William Sr., wasn't home yet but I couldn't wait for him to see my encore prime-time performance of the crowning achievement.

Getting my mom to notice the report card was hard work. I got my accolades and now I was actually thirsty. As I turned around to get the OJ, my mom nonchalantly tossed out one more line over her shoulder as she headed toward the living room: "Looking at your grades, if you tried a little harder, you probably could have made all A's." Then she walked away. Dang. She just left it right there. I turned around to ask, "Say whut?" But she was already gone. She just dropped the mic and exited stage left.

She put that thought in my head and I instantly went from "Look at me, William Packer, world dominator and honor roll student!" to "Well, wait a minute, could I really make all A's? Like, is that a real thing? Were those dean's list losers *that* much better than me?" It hadn't crossed my mind until that moment as something I should even necessarily be striving for. I was just fine with what I had done. Now I started to question *everything*. Was I even trying in school? I went from thinking how cool it was to *make* the honor roll to thinking what a tragedy it was that I had *missed* the dean's list.

Basically, my mom had just said, "William, you ain't that great . . . but you could be."

It was like the movie *Inception*. She had gone deep into my subconscious and left this little idea of me being a complete abject failure in life, then went to catch *Phil Donahue*. That simple sentence had a profound effect on me. In that moment, I realized two things:

1. I wasn't even thirsty anymore. The whole refrigerator ruse was a bust. And I had risked my family's well-being letting our precious cold air escape in the process.
2. My mom was absolutely right. Moms always are. It had never crossed my mind because at that time I hadn't set up this idea of defining success by the dean's list. I was defining success by whatever the school told me was successful. So when my teacher said, "Little William, you're amazing, you did great," that was good enough for me.

My mom had the audacity to say, "You're even greater than that. You could be *really* great." She didn't take away what I had done. And she didn't say any of the things that my subconscious was telling me about how my life was a failure at nine years old. She gave me all the accolades and then proposed that one idea and walked away. I was like, "Hmmm, is that a challenge?" I thought about the extra-credit assignments I could've done but didn't. I thought about additional time I could've spent studying for tests but didn't. Then I thought, "I will show her. The next time grades come out I will have a full-blown straight-A celebration in this kitchen, with a marching band, mascots, and a refrigerator door hanging wide open for hours!" {*Narrator: Now, you know this is a whole lie. That fridge door is staying closed.*}

From that point on, I was self-motivated in a different way. I was now trying to be the absolute best of the best when it came to elementary school academics. I made straight A's from then on, I rose to the top of my class, and I began the foundation of a work ethic that borders on perfectionism that still serves me to this day (and makes some people crazy, but we'll get into that later).

As I've discussed, people who achieve greatness realize it doesn't matter how well you do something if you don't finish the damn deal. And don't just finish it. Finish it strong. And how strong you finish is only limited by the amount of work you're willing to put into it. This is true in life and it's true in moviemaking. My movie *Think Like a Man,* based on Steve Harvey's bestseller, shot out of the gate at the box-office opening weekend and was projected to be number one instantly, even though it hadn't even opened on the West Coast yet. Watching those first box-office numbers come in is nerve-racking; they trickle in from all over the country. Based on what a movie does at noon on Friday in New York, they extrapolate the data to estimate the total box-office number for the whole weekend. The studio data crunchers use an algorithm and they update it hourly.

I knew going into the weekend we had a chance to be the number-one movie. I put my heart and soul into that movie opening. I had taken my cast to various theaters to pop up and surprise audiences by taking selfies and handing out movie swag. I had called in favors with other celebs to do coordinated social media posts to help raise the volume of conversation. We were one of the first movies to employ these tactics. I had done all the legwork it took to make a blockbuster. By Friday night, I was feeling so good, I was sure we had a big ol' hit on our hands.

I called Steve Harvey that night. "We're going to make twenty million dollars!" I exclaimed. "We're going to make our budget back on opening night!"

"Wow, Pack! That's amazing, brother. I'm proud of you, man. You busted your ass on this movie."

"I appreciate you, Unk," I replied.

"Is it over?"

"What do you mean?"

"Well, you said we're gonna make twenty million. That's awesome, but it's just Friday night. Could it go higher?"

"Well, the way it works, that number is an estimate for the entire weekend based on what we made today," I explained.

"I get that," he said. "What if Saturday and Sunday are even bigger than they estimate? Could it go higher than twenty million?"

"Ummm, yeah, I guess it could."

"Well, no matter what, you did great, man. Congrats! Let me know what else I can do to help."

The conversation with Steve lit a fire under me and made me feel like, as hard as I had worked, maybe I hadn't done enough. So at midnight on Friday, I called all the cast members (several of whom *may* have been drunk and celebrating by then) and said, "We're doing more pop-ups tomorrow night. Who can go to the Grove? Who can go downtown? Who can go to the Palisades?" I called Steve back and told him I needed him to pop up too. Steve, Kevin Hart, Taraji Henson, Terrence J, Regina Hall, Gab Union, La La, Meagan Good, Mike Ealy, Jerry Ferrara, Romany Malco, Gary Owen, and so many others went the extra mile. By the time the actual numbers came in, we had made over $33 million opening weekend. The extra work paid off.

The additional energy spent that takes something from being good to being great is transformative. It's all that really matters. As a filmmaker, it doesn't matter if I've got a great idea. It doesn't matter if I've got the right actor and the right director. I haven't done anything until I've shot the movie, edited it, distributed it, marketed it, and, by the way, not just completed those things but done them really, really well.

Sometimes it can feel so daunting to accomplish a difficult task that getting the thing done feels like success enough. Maybe. But probably not. If you need to take a break, breathe, and recalibrate— do that. Then get right back at it and challenge yourself to push past good into great. The first step is being honest about the fact that you can do better. That can be a painful conversation to have, even if it's just you with you. It can feel like you're being too hard on yourself and not giving yourself enough credit. But really what you're saying is, "Self. We're good. We're really good. Now how can we be *great*?!" Try having that conversation the next time you accomplish a goal. Maybe not aloud in public though. Try it in the privacy of your own home. Like in the kitchen, in front of a closed refrigerator door.

4

The Fortuitous No

The Art of the Pivot

One of the worst sounds in the world is someone telling you no. And I don't mean let-you-down-easy, it's-not-you-it's-me, maybe-next-time soft declines. I'm talking in-your-face, no-holds-barred repudiation. I know because I have had my share. I've also learned that the well-worn phrase is true: A *no* can be a blessing in disguise. Rejection forces you to do one of two things: crawl into a ball of self-loathing and despair while crying "Why me, Lord?!" to the heavens, *or* . . . pivot. Do something else that just might ultimately be the right path forward. Getting turned down stings and can make it hard to see anything but the pain of the rejection. But if you can put aside your sensitivities and your ego and focus on regrouping, a *no* could be one of the best things ever to happen to you.

Shortly after graduation I had moved to Atlanta and was trying to get my film career going. I desperately wanted to make a movie called *The Bottom,* about a music artist in the southern booty-shaking bass music genre that originated in Miami and was very popular throughout the Southeast at the time. *Bottom* is not only slang for bass, but in Florida if people ask, "Where you from?" and you say, "The Bottom," they know you mean Miami because geographically it sits at the bottom of the state. I really thought this film was going to be our generation's *Purple Rain* or *8 Mile.* I was trying to raise $5 million from investors, which was crazy high for where I was on the Hollywood totem pole, literally the bottom. I'm telling you now, I wasn't prepared to produce at that budget level at that time. I simply wasn't ready. I would have blown the money. Not on a fleet of Benzes or anything like that, I just was not experienced enough to know how to manage the finances of a production on that scale.

But I was so desperate for a green light on this project because I literally had nothing else going on with my film career. I had gotten shut out trying to produce music videos, and Hollywood, shockingly, still wasn't returning my calls. I had long since graduated with an engineering degree that was gathering dust on the shelf. The money was running low. This felt like life or death. So you can understand how crushed I was when I got a resounding *no* across the board. Now, in hindsight, I'm thankful I didn't get that money because it would have tanked my career and defined me as a guy nobody should ever give money to again. It was a *Fortuitous No.* But you could not tell me that at the time. Those rejections cut deep. I started to really question whether this film thing was even for me. I needed to figure out a backup plan.

I'd been a really popular DJ on the campus station in college. The way the station was set up, it played jazz during the day and then went to an open format where the DJs could play what they wanted at night. My night was Thursday, and I killed it. No other station in the city came close to my audience during my time slot. I had great song selection and a great *DJ voice.* I was the energetic guy who spoke in a hyper tone and barely took a breath:

"*SupTallyHOInTheMeantimeBetweentimeIt'sYoursTrulayYour*

*NumberOneDJHourAfterHourFromTheWAMFTowerIt'sDJWILL
POWER!"* I was that guy.

> *{Narrator: *Ahem* The world is really lucky Will Packer became
> successful making movies.}*

When I couldn't get *The Bottom* off the ground, I put together
an air check, basically a demo of the greatest hits of DJ Willpower
from my Tallahassee days. I knew a guy, who knew a guy, who
worked at V-103, which was the biggest station in Atlanta. I figured I would probably have to work my way up to a coveted slot like
morning show host, so I told my connect, "I'm *willing* to start on the
overnight shift." I figured for someone of my considerable talents
and reach they would jump at the chance to have *me* on in the middle of the night. The feedback I got from the radio guy was that my
air check was just "all right." Excuse me?

"Dude," I explained, "I'm not asking for the afternoon drive.
I'm trying to help you out. I am willing to come on from two A.M.
to six A.M. when nobody is listening. I'm Will Packer from FAMU,
DJ Willpower! I'm bringing hundreds—and I mean hundreds—of
fans who will tune in just because I'm on the air."

"Yeah, we get thousands of these air checks that we throw
away every day. Most of them better than this one." Pain. Humbled.
Ashamed. The one thing that I didn't even really *want* to do but that
I *knew* I could do really well, and I couldn't even get taken seriously
in that medium. What was I doing with my life?

It turned out to be another Fortuitous No. That Fortuitous
No on top of *The Bottom* Fortuitous No forced me to change course
completely. I ended up pivoting to make an entirely different independent film, the psychological thriller *Trois,* for a more reasonable
$75,000. That is what I needed to be making at that time. Not a
multimillion-dollar music movie and not playing quiet storm records on an overnight shift. *Trois* ended up making a million dollars

at the box office and was my—say it with me in my Willpower radio voice—"*long-awaited, highly anticipated, totally legitimated*" entry into the Hollywood club. *Trois* opened up doors.

There are times in life that a *no* will make you work that much harder for a *yes.* A Fortuitous No can make you reassess your goals and often push you to find a more creative way of getting where you're trying to go.

After *Trois,* Rob Hardy and I set out to make a movie called *Stomp the Yard* about fraternity culture and step competitions at a Black college. I knew I would need Hollywood financing, and all the major studios were in L.A. But these were still very broke days and we couldn't afford to fly across the country. So I got my hands on some buddy passes on Southwest Airlines, then on travel day we would get to the airport at six A.M. and wait all day if necessary for a buddy pass–eligible ("non-revenue," they're called) seat to open up so we could make the cross-country trek.

Rob and I met with anybody who would take a meeting. Even still we could not get a single studio in Hollywood to buy in to this idea. They all passed. Every last one said, "No, thank you."

We flew back home to Atlanta with our heads bloodied but unbowed. Still broke. But we refused to give up. My gut told me there had to be a way to get this movie made. In this situation, it didn't matter how many times we got told *no,* we knew we only needed one *yes.* And basically this was a last stand. If we weren't able to get this movie going, there was no plan B. Plan A *had* to work. At the time I was working for *The Atlanta Journal-Constitution* delivering newspapers door-to-door from three A.M. to six A.M., and then turning around and selling newspaper subscriptions from four P.M. to seven P.M. I scraped enough money together from both newspaper jobs to buy another couple buddy passes (yes, airline employees sell these) and fly back to L.A. This was a very big risk. We didn't have the resources to keep flying across the country with no results.

We walked back into the same rooms. How did we get back

into those same rooms? Glad you asked, dear reader. We would either pitch a different person or tell them we were pitching a different movie. {Narrator: It was the same movie.}

We pitched it again because we were relentless. We wouldn't give up. "Weren't you just in here? Didn't we just tell you no?" we heard more than a few times. I think we thought our sheer persistence and resilience would buy us some goodwill and they might reconsider the project. No and no.

However, there was one place we thought we had a chance—and all it takes is one. It wasn't that they wanted to make my movie *Stomp the Yard;* in fact, a junior exec said to me with a straight face, "I think this Black college stepping movie that you're trying to make is a bad idea. First of all, like . . . can we talk about Black colleges. Is that really a thing?" Then he whispered conspiratorially, "I don't know where you guys are from, but you know you can get into real colleges, right? You guys gotta try harder!" He actually said that.

You know the smile you give when you're in pain and it's not really a smile but more like you're baring your teeth? I gave him that look and said, "I wonder why we didn't think of that." He didn't catch any sarcasm. He was so proud, like he had just walked into an antebellum-era NAACP meeting with the secret to freedom.

But before I could really be a smart-ass, this fella said, "I doubt that movie's going to fly, but one of our most successful movies last year was this dance movie *You Got Served.*" They had made it for around $7 million and it made $50 million. It wasn't that $50 million was all the money in the world from a Hollywood perspective, but the movie industry, like most industries, is all about profit margins. That was a *huge* return. "We've been trying to figure out a sequel to *You Got Served,*" he said. The lightbulb went on over my precious little HBCU-bred head.

I called an audible. I didn't pitch a Black college movie. I didn't pitch a movie about fraternities and sororities. I didn't pitch a movie about stepping. You know what I pitched? I pitched a sequel to *You Got Served*. And in this sequel, one of the guys from *You Got Served* was going to hook up with a dance crew in another part of the country and bring his style of dance and combine it with the style of dance that these people were used to. The studio said, "I love it! Now you're talking!" And of course what we did was make that "new style" of dance stepping, and the new guys were in a fraternity, and the new environment was a Black college. And that's the story of how I got *Stomp the Yard* a green light. And it ended up number one at the box office for two weeks in a row.

Here's the kicker: In Hollywood, once you're successful, everybody goes, "Who the bleep is that? Who is this person who came outta nowhere with a hit movie? Get 'em on the phone." Every last one of those studios that had passed, who gave me a Fortuitous No, called me and said, "Hey, why didn't you pitch us this *Stomp the Yard* movie? We would've made that, and we would've made it better."

You know what I said? "You guys gotta try harder."

Lesson is, after I was told no, I was malleable. I figured out the environment, I figured out the rules of engagement, and I adjusted. Sometimes you've got to be a little Machiavellian, in an "ends justify the means" kind of way. I still was able to accomplish what I wanted to accomplish, but I had to do it in a way that was palatable for this particular industry. In this case, it was movie studios who had an aversion to telling the story the way I wanted to tell it. So I gave them what they thought they wanted, and I still was able to tell a version of the story I wanted to tell.

A Fortuitous No can make you work a hell of a lot harder for a *yes*. Sometimes you have to determine the cost of that *yes*. An executive named Clint Culpepper at Sony Pictures approached me with the idea for the movie *Obsessed*. It was a thrilling concept— a provocative twist on *Fatal Attraction*—a hybrid featuring a Black couple stalked by a white woman. I was excited about the opportunity. The studio made it clear that the concept was strong enough that the film could move forward without being dependent on any particular cast member.

At that time, I already had a great relationship with Idris Elba, whom I had worked with on his first theatrical film after he finished his run on *The Wire*: an independent faith-based movie called *The Gospel*. Side note: My mom inspired me to make *The Gospel* because up till then I had only been able to get financing to make erotic thrillers. My mom said, "Why don't you make something I can take my church missionary sisters to?" I got you, Ma. *{Narrator: What his mother didn't tell him but he learned later was that she and all her church sisters faithfully went to see every erotic movie Will had ever made. And they loved them! Praise God.}*

It was obvious that Idris Elba was a Hollywood star waiting to blow. And so, with that in mind, I thought about who could bring even more star power to the film. Beyoncé came to mind, and through her agent, I reached out to her. To my surprise, Beyoncé was actually looking to do a project just like this. It seemed like the perfect fit. She had done *The Fighting Temptations* and *Austin Powers in Goldmember* and *Dreamgirls,* but this would be her first thriller.

I sent Beyoncé the script, hoping that she would be as enthusiastic about *Obsessed* as I was.

But when she responded, she said she liked the idea, was flattered that I had approached her, but she politely declined. It was disheartening, but I respected her decision. I moved forward, discussing other actresses who could potentially fill the role.

Then something unexpected happened. Word got back to the studio that Beyoncé liked the concept but passed on the project, and suddenly, they insisted that the movie needed her star power. All of a sudden having Beyoncé on board had become a necessity. Just the possibility of Beyoncé being in this movie made the studio change their minds—now they'd only green-light it if somehow *she* said yes.

"What? I thought you guys liked the concept so much it didn't matter who starred in it."

"Yeah, but we like it *a whole lot more* with Beyoncé in it."

I went from having a "go" movie at Sony to having a movie that only one of the biggest stars on the planet could get green-lit. I knew the cost of the *yes* was going to be high, but it would be worth it because otherwise I would lose the movie.

At times the cost of a *yes* is not worth it. A very famous actress wanted the role of scene-stealer Dina in *Girls Trip* but was asking for too much money. I wouldn't have been able to pay the rest of the cast if I had agreed to that. We instead cast a new rising star named Tiffany Haddish, and it ended up being her breakout role and launched her into the stratosphere. That famous actress still regrets not taking that role to this day. She told me so. I have a few folks like that.

I went back to Beyoncé, and we had an honest conversation about her reservations. She liked the script but didn't love it. There were certain elements she wanted to change and adjust to make it a version of the movie she could fully embrace. I found myself in a tough spot. I had to make a choice—stick with the original script that the financier, director, other actors, and I liked . . . *or* do whatever it took to accommodate Beyoncé's vision.

With my back against the wall, I told Beyoncé that I would work on the script to address her concerns. She made it clear she didn't want me to alter it solely for her sake, which is a nice way of saying, "Change the script if you want to. I'm still not promising I'm gonna do the movie." I assured her that I believed I could make the changes in a way that would make the movie even better. She was honest and kind but reiterated she couldn't guarantee that she would ultimately say yes to the project, so she suggested I make the movie I thought was best. "Ummm, you in it is the movie I think is best," I thought but didn't say out loud.

Undeterred, I dove back into the script with the writer, removing every issue Beyoncé had raised. I wanted to give her a version of the movie that she could genuinely connect with while protecting the overall vision. When I presented her with the revised script, she acknowledged that I had done everything she asked for. Even still, she came back and said, "No, I'm sorry. I can't do *Obsessed.* I'm not gonna do it."

This was a major letdown. But I just couldn't take no for an answer. I knew I needed to keep removing reasons for her to say no. Tour schedule too busy? Okay. Got it. Listen, when does she have time? Throughout my career I've worked with touring artists a lot. I've done movies with Kevin Hart, Ludacris, Chris Brown, and others. Their schedules are always insane.

Don't like the script? We'll get a new writer.

Director rub you the wrong way? He's gone.

She had major reservations due to her busy schedule. She had makeup and hair product promotional campaigns and a tour on the horizon, making it nearly impossible to find a window of time.

Beyoncé passed on *Obsessed* five times. "Tell Will he's great, lovely meeting him, but it's not going to work," she said through her people.

Drawing from my past experiences working with music artists, I asked her team for the number of consecutive days she had available, not expecting her to have much flexibility. I said I understand she's passing but give me the dates anyway just so I can take a look at the schedule. We managed to create a crazy schedule set around her tour and promotional schedule, we reconfigured blocks of time, adjusted our work weeks, and found a way to make it work. Once again, I presented the plan to Beyoncé, demonstrating that I had eliminated every reason for her to say no to the project. She appreciated the effort and acknowledged that I had gone above and beyond. Still, she hesitated. But after meeting with the studio, potential directors, and Idris, she finally started to engage in the possibility. And I had laid out a blueprint for how it could work schedule-wise.

She finally said yes.

Whatever the issue was that kept her saying no, I removed it. I was dogged. My studio exec Clint Culpepper supported all my crazy accommodations, 100 percent. And guess what. It was all worth it. *Obsessed* was a smash, opening as the number-one movie in the country, and was my biggest domestic hit to date.

A *no* can be a blessing in disguise because it forces us to fine-tune our approach. If you get told no and you don't give up, you're gonna come out the other side of the experience stronger for it. Because now when you attack the challenge again, you will be even better prepared because you will have removed the reasons for the first *no*.

A harsh denial can feel like the worst thing ever, but sometimes you end up in a better place. Instead of focusing on the failure, ask yourself how to turn it into a Fortuitous No. Try focusing on the fact that there is a *yes* out there somewhere. The *yes* may or may not be in the same area where you got the *no*. Instead of spending time in a space you weren't supposed to be putting energy into, now you can search for the *yes*. Easy? No way. Worth it? Abso-freaking-lutely. In the voice of that clueless exec who unwittingly helped me get *Stomp the Yard* made: You just gotta try harder.

WHY DO WE GET FIXATED ON THE DOOR THAT'S CLOSED?

Getting a Fortuitous No sometimes means you gotta kick in doors. And it means you can't waste time on excuses for why the door is closed in the first place. In elementary school, I got transferred into the gifted class. After the first day, I came home ranting to my parents about how bad and racist it was. Nothing happened, mind you, but I was the only Black kid and I felt like everybody was staring at me. I hated it. My parents let me have my little first-grade tantrum, then they said, "Okay, now let us tell you how good you got it being the only Black kid in the gifted class. When you walk in, you've got everybody's attention. Take it and run with it. Never give it up. All eyes are on you. It's up to you to decide what you do with it. All the other white kids have to do something extra to stand out. They may indeed be racist, they may think that you are less than, they may not want to give you a fair shake. Doesn't matter. Go, and outperform them."

Sometimes we get so fixated on what's wrong and what's not fair. That's the closed door. Your job is to find a way in, at any cost. If the front door is locked, go to the back door. If that door is locked, climb through the window. If the window's locked, cut a hole in the roof. Just get in. No. Matter. What.

There are a lot of people who will spend a lot of time yelling at that closed door, writing think pieces about the lock, putting up signs and banners lamenting who installed the door. That's one method, and we need those voices. However, I've always been someone who says, "That is absolutely not fair!" *while* I'm looking for another way in. It's been my experience that those who ultimately win and get ahead are the ones who find the other opening while others are still arguing about why that door is closed. Just make sure you go back and unlock it once you get in.

5

Boy, You Wild

Use What Motivates Others to Your Advantage

What happens right after people take a group picture? Everyone rushes to review it, right, lest the moment pass and a bad picture somehow makes its way online, ruining lives for all posterity. And what happens when they review the picture? Do they look at all the folks in it? No. They zoom right in to themselves, right past you, past the great pyramids of Egypt or whichever wonder of the world they're standing in front of. They zoom right to the wrinkle in their slacks or whatever the thing is that always bothers them about their appearance. Then all they can say is, "No, no, no. Don't post this. We have to take another one."

If you want to connect with anyone anywhere, find out very early on, "What's that person's wrinkle in their slacks?" What makes them tick? Floats their boat? Gets them out of bed in the morning? You have to read people. People's favorite subject is very often themselves. People always want to talk about themselves. People always want to tell you what they need. People always want to tell you what they've done. Use that to your advantage. Be willing to pay attention and listen, and it's not that hard to find out what's important to them. Listen way more than you talk. In conversations, resist the urge to just wait for the moment to interject about *your* favorite subject, which, by the way, is probably yourself.

People *{Narrator: Will's mom}* often say I wasted my engineering degree. Au contraire, I feel it gave me a leg up on my peers. It forced me to hone my analytical mind. The engineering discipline teaches you to approach problem-solving analytically. It takes time to hone the step-by-step process of deductive reasoning and analyzing problems based on an unemotional examination of the data at hand. But once you get it down it can be invaluable in a variety of areas.

I've got a lot of practice sharpening those skills because making movies is all about solving problems. At any given moment, I can be overseeing fifteen to twenty projects in various stages. I'm constantly getting calls about what's going on with these projects. I can count on one hand how many times over my three-decade career I've gotten a call that sounded like "Nothing is wrong. I just wanted to let you know that everything is going *great*!" I don't get those calls. When I get called, it's to attempt to put out some seventeen-alarm fire. Most times the problems I'm trying to solve have nothing to do with malfunctioning equipment or error-prone technology. Most times it has to do with some issue revolving around people. I've learned that the best way to problem-solve around issues involving humans is to try to get out in front of them *before* they become major. I try to anticipate and head off conflict before it reaches a critical level. That means I have to figure out what's important to key people on every movie. Certainly with every actor, writer, and director. It is a creative industry with a lot of delicate egos, so I spend a lot of time trying to figure out what motivates people.

I learned this lesson the hard way growing up. There was a time when I was in high school when I was not perceptive enough to determine what was important to two very different friends of mine. I had a football teammate we called D-Mack. *{Narrator: I'm pretty sure Will has changed this name.}* We both attended St. Petersburg High, which was on the north side of town. The north side of St. Pete was the predominantly white side of town. Our school was mostly well-off white students and a small percentage of Black kids who were bused in, many from south-side housing projects. Now, I lived on the south side and wasn't zoned for this school, but St. Pete High also had an International Baccalaureate program. I was always very academically astute, so I was accepted into the IB program and off to St. Pete High I went. I thrived in high school academically and socially. I graduated number three in my class. Making friends with the upper-middle-class white kids while maintaining my relationships with the homies on the south side is how I ended up becoming student body president and Mr. St. Pete High at this very white school.

I made the white kids *and* the Black kids part of my crew. My fellow south-side homeboy D-Mack and I had a lot in common but were very different dudes. We both played football, lived on the same side of town, and of course attended the same school. But that's pretty much where it ended. D-Mack had a lengthy criminal record by the time he entered high school. He was the kind of kid who started growing a beard when he was in second grade. D-Mack was that guy. Nobody messed with D-Mack. He dressed in designer clothes at all times and had a mouth full of gold teeth that were always shiny. But even though I wasn't from his world, we were tight. He understood that I was a sheltered middle-class kid, and I knew he was a real street dude, so he would always put me up on game about how to navigate the streets.

We were the only kids at our school with donks. If you don't know what a donk is, it's a highly coveted old-school full-sized sedan (usually made by Chevrolet) that has been customized with rims, a sound system, and a paint job. D-Mack's donk was sitting on gold

Dayton rims with a candy paint job. I, on the other hand, had an old-school Oldsmobile Cutlass Supreme with neither paint job nor fancy rims. Honestly, my car was probably more of a hooptie than a donk, but now we're just splitting urban car label hairs. All my car really needed was a few coats of paint, mechanical work, wheels, and a rear window. That's all. And not like the whole back window, just one rear side window. Basically, it needed a rear quarter glass—that's the small triangular window some cars used to have that could be tilted open. Mine was missing.

D-Mack was obsessed with my inoperable window and always reminded me that it needed fixing. I honestly couldn't tell if he was roasting me or offering friendly advice. Then again, I also don't know how a dope boy who could grow a five-o'clock shadow by the end of second lunch somehow fell under the spell of the whitest white girl in the history of white girls. Her name was Maddy. *{Narrator: Will has definitely changed this name.}*

As you probably deduced from her name, Maddy was the kind of girl who dotted every letter *i* with a heart, was a cheerleader, and loved pink. Although I had never been to her house, I imagined that she had a life-sized dollhouse and a furry dog with a human name like Bartholomew or Priscilla and her mom had a lot of casserole dishes. Maddy was the prototypical girl next door, but not next to the doors where D-Mack and I lived on the south side, where most Maddys feared to tread.

But Maddy was a fearless rich white girl. She wasn't like what we call a "Karen" today. It didn't matter if you were white, Black, Asian, whatever. She hung with everybody and she was very comfortable in her own skin. That's why everybody loved her and a lot of dudes had a crush on her. If I'm being totally honest, I probably did too. But she didn't like me like that. We were legitimately just cool.

I don't know if it had something to do with a scarcity of Black people on her side of town, but Maddy was enamored with Black culture. She would always ask to hang with me on the "Black" side of town. One day after football practice during one of our conversations about my missing quarter glass, D-Mack confided in me that he had a crush on Maddy. And that's when I made one of the stupidest decisions I had made since deciding to play high school football. *{Narrator: Will was like 125 pounds. It made no sense for him to play football. In the athletic hotbed of Florida, no less. He has neck problems to this day.}*

One Friday I decided to surprise D-Mack by bringing Maddy to his house. She was ecstatic. D-Mack was a mythical figure at school, and for someone who lived in north St. Pete, going to his house was like going to fantasy thug camp or smoking weed with Snoop Dogg—a privileged suburban kid's dream.

We hopped into my certified donk, and Maddy squirmed with excitement as we cruised over to the south side of town, soaking up the details so she could relay the story of her hood adventure to her friends. I didn't call. I didn't page D-Mack. I planned to pull up to his mama's house with Malibu Barbie in the front seat of my car and ring the doorbell for no other reason than to flex and show this white girl that I knew where the cool Black guys lived.

D-Mack and I may have lived on the same side of town, but my actual neighborhood was a squarely middle-class area, while his would be generously called "working-class." As we approached, the shirtless tatted dudes hanging on porch stoops and clothes hanging from clotheslines swaying in the wind let Maddy know she wasn't in Kansas anymore.

We pulled up and the house looked a mess. There was a couch in the front yard that looked like it had been there for quite some time. It looked completely unusable except for the fact that it was currently being used by a drunk dude who was sleeping on it. There were three old donks out front in various states of disrepair. Some had chipped rims, some had busted windows, none looked drivable. I convinced D-Mack to come outside by telling him that I had a friend with me. When he realized who was sitting in my car, D-Mack squinted as if he was hallucinating. He looked at me and peered back toward my front seat to make sure he wasn't imagining this scenario. Then he looked at me *again* and then *back* to the front seat. Now, D-Mack was a badass. I had never seen him blush. I'm willing to bet he had never blushed in his life. By definition, that's a hard thing to gauge with Black people anyway. But I tell you, I saw this dark-skinned, African American, colored Negro *blush* when he realized Maddy was in his front yard! Meanwhile, D-Mack's mom was in the yard hanging clothes on the clothesline, screaming at him to close the door before he let all the cold air out.

"What is you *doing?*" he asked me.

I slowly began to realize my mistake. You can't just pop up on someone at their mother's house without warning. I mean, I could if I was solo but not with a living American Girl doll in tow. D-Mack had carefully constructed an image of how he wanted to be seen, and I was pulling back the veil and ruining it. I had invaded his home environs. D-Mack smiled uncomfortably at Maddy. Maddy couldn't stop looking around at *everything* like it was a *National Geographic* opened to a page with naked natives. It was cringey. As the embarrassment began to sweep over me, D-Mack uttered the only sentence appropriate for the moment:

"Boy, you wild."

In African American vernacular, "Boy, you wild" is the Black equivalent of "My gosh!" with a little bit of "Well, I never!" and "Newsflash, buddy" sprinkled in. It is both an exclamation and a warning. It is a song of sorrow and a Negro spiritual. It's what Lincoln said to John Wilkes Booth when he saw him climbing a curtain at Ford's Theatre. When God found Adam wearing a fig leaf and eating from the Tree of Knowledge of Good and Evil fruit salad, I bet he said, "Adam! Boy, you wild!"

The interaction was relatively quick and uneventful. Five minutes after we pulled up, D-Mack's mom yelled for him to come do something in the house, and he said quickly, "I'll see y'all at school Monday." I should have known right then that he was furious. As I drove off, I noticed a slump in D-Mack's shoulders as he walked into his house. Maddy continued to look around the neighborhood in wild-eyed amazement, and I started having second thoughts as I drove into the afternoon traffic with Maddy from the Block by my side.

I spent the weekend contemplating whether I should apologize to D-Mack but then thought perhaps I was overthinking it. When Monday came around, I decided to gauge his reaction when I saw him during seventh period. I got dressed, headed out the door to school, and . . . wait, something feels different. It was a little chilly for a Florida morning, but that wasn't it. I realized I had forgotten to bring the trash can up from the side of the road like my dad had told me to, but it wasn't that either. Something was off. . . . Wait, what happened to my car? I stood there in the driveway and realized that my entire automobile was missing.

I ran inside and informed my parents that someone had absconded with my beloved donk. After their initial confusion and wondering why I was hyperventilating about a missing mule, I was finally able to convey to my parents that I was not talking about a donk*ey* but that my car had been stolen. Of course, I wanted to call the FBI, Homeland Security, and, if possible, Interpol, but my father was much smarter than me. He made me promise not to tell anyone. I'm sorry, what? He said, "We'll file a police report and then I'll take you to school. But when you get there don't mention this to anyone."

I was confused but I heeded my father's words and remained quiet all day. During first period no one even noticed I hadn't driven to school. During second period, I saw Maddy still bathing in her hood bliss, but nothing was out of the ordinary. I think I was expecting that the whole school would've noticed somehow that I didn't have my car, but everyone had the audacity to go about their lives like normal. At lunchtime, there wasn't even the slightest rumor spreading about my car. By sixth period, I realized no one was organizing a prayer vigil with candles pushed through paper plates or even offering their thoughts and prayers for my missing prized possession. In the last period of the day, D-Mack walked up to me. I was prepared to get smashed in the face for my pop-up Maddy stunt, but instead D-Mack put his hands on my shoulders and, with all sincerity, said, "Man, I'm so sorry to hear about your car."

I hadn't told a soul. No one else knew about my car. It didn't take an International Baccalaureate student to deduce that my homie jacked my car as revenge for bringing Maddy to his house.

A few days later, the cops called to tell my dad they had found my pride and joy sitting in what can only be described as "the cut." The seats were ripped apart. The speakers that I had bought with my life savings were gone. The rims and tires were in the wind. Nothing was intact . . . except for the windows. Somehow, they had stolen the car without breaking a window. When the cops explained to my dad that the missing rear quarter glass made it super easy for them to gain access to the car and hot-wire the steering wheel, I just listened stoically.

My father eventually helped me restore my car back to drivable condition, but D-Mack and I were never the same. Ultimately, I realized that I was the one who had violated the relationship between us. I was trying to flex, and my impromptu ambush robbed him of the carefully constructed image he had maintained throughout high school. Maddy would never again see him as the hood legend whose gold chains swooped over his football jersey when he hopped into his top-of-the-line donk. He was a mortal.

I found the wrinkle in D-Mack's slacks.

D-Mack was embarrassed by the whole thing. Even worse, as a middle-class Black kid, I hadn't considered that D-Mack might not want his white classmates to know how different his life was when he wasn't at school. I had actually murdered his persona—and I did it with a person who mattered to him. {Narrator: Dumbass.}

Lesson: You have to be more perceptive than everyone else and prioritize learning to read people. Just as important, don't be a show-off. Something that serves me well in this wild industry with many different kinds of people is spending a lot of time trying to figure out what everyone's motivation is. When you're trying to put a team together, if you figure out what each person thinks they want or thinks they need and you listen and you're perceptive, you will be better able to get everybody on your team working for your overall goal.

I was not perceptive enough to determine what was important to D-Mack, what was important to Maddy, and what was important to me, then execute on that in a way that worked for everyone. I totally misread that room. And it backfired on me.

It seems like I'm telling you to pay attention to other people, give other people what they want, and be sensitive to other people's needs, which I am. But all of that is in service to the ultimate goal: working with people to accomplish *your* objective. Tie their goal in to yours. Find out what's important to people, then use that to position it as a win-win situation. If Maddy's goal was to get a behind-the-scenes look into a slice of life she didn't have access to, I could've conspired with D-Mack to make that happen in a way that maintained his image. I still would have been the guy who made that happen for Maddy.

I should end this by revealing that D-Mack married Maddy, and if you ride through south St. Pete on a clear night, you can still see Maddy hanging out clothes with Mama Mack. But that wouldn't be true. At all. I found Maddy on Facebook a few years back and she seems to be living comfortably and quite unaffected by her southside adventures. I don't know what happened to D-Mack. He could be a state senator in Pennsylvania, and he could be in the state pen.

It doesn't matter. What matters is that Maddy learned that D-Mack is not a stereotype or a meme defined by gold chains and bass music but a real human being. D-Mack learned how to boost cars and where to hide them. And I learned that if this whole movie biz thing implodes, my next career should not be matchmaker.

By the way, a few months after that incident, D-Mack came up to me and asked if they ever caught the guys who stole my car. I just looked at him and gave the one and only response I could: "Boy, you wild."

THE NEIGHBORS THINK I'M SELLING DOPE

I didn't really hang with the white kids from my school on the weekends. Not because they didn't invite me to, just because it seemed all they did was party and drink and I didn't drink in high school. Also my parents wouldn't let me hang out late. The white kids were kind of unforgiving about that. Whereas the Black kids were like, "We get it. We got Black mamas too. What time do you need to be home? We got you," the white kids would be like, "Dude, come on! The party doesn't even start till midnight! And Catherine better not be bitching when I get home!"

"Ummm, who's Catherine?"

"My mom!"

Yeahhhh, okay.

So one weekend before I had my donk/hooptie, I was driving my mom's minivan. I had just picked up my friends who happened to live in the projects. It was Mark, Eric, Dennis, and me. That was the crew. We were leaving Eric's house in the projects when the police lights hit us. I pulled over immediately and the cops made us get out of the car. Now, when I was growing up, whenever any of my white friends got pulled over, the cops came up, they'd check their license and registration, and if they did something wrong, maybe got a stern talking to or, worst case, a ticket and they were on their way. Black kids? For us, most times we'd have to get out of the car and often get on the ground or put our hands on the hood of the car. Which is always alarming because you never know what's going to happen. This was waaayyyy before George Floyd and cellphone cameras.

So the police made us get out of the car and get on the ground. As I'm getting down I kept hearing my dad saying, "If you're in an interaction with the police, always be polite. Don't raise your voice. Do whatever they say. Don't make them feel threatened. De-escalate." Otherwise known in the Black community as "The Talk." I was completely compliant because that's what my parents told me to do. And although I hadn't done anything wrong, I was nervous. The other kids, especially Eric, were mad.

"Why we gotta get on the ground?" Eric fumed. "Why you messing with us?"

What often happens in these situations when one cop pulls you over, other cops just start showing up out of nowhere. Before I knew it, I looked up and there were six cop cars with lights flashing. It was frightening. The other cops who pulled up are ostensibly just backing up the initial officers. But it's also an intentional show of force and intimidation.

For middle-class Will Packer, who had never even gotten a traffic ticket before, it was terrifying. All four of us were on the ground and there was now a football team of amped-up cops surrounding us. Mark and I were quiet. Eric and Dennis were shouting, "This is messed up. Why you got us on the ground?! We didn't do anything wrong!"

"Whose car is this?" one of the cops barked.

"Sir, it's my mom's car," I said.

"Sure," his words said. His tone said, "Four Black dudes leaving the projects in a minivan? Yeah, right!" He wasn't buying it. The implication was clear.

"Did you steal this car?"

"No, sir."

I wanted to explain that I didn't have a car, and this is what my mom drives. I can't help that she's not cool. Meanwhile, Eric and Dennis were still yelling and complaining and mad. And I was whispering, "Shut up. Shut up. Chill. Don't make this any worse."

This was becoming a very dangerous situation. These officers were doing anything *but* de-escalating. Imagine: You're on the ground, and they're telling you not to move. Your friends are mad. The cops are yelling. I just kept thinking, "Please don't let one of my friends move too fast. Please don't let a gun accidentally go off." You just don't know what's going to happen. And I'll never forget the feeling of cold hard asphalt on my face and the little gravel biting into my cheek. It feels like it's cutting your face. But you don't dare get up and wipe it off. You're uncomfortable. You're scared to move. You're a Black kid, and you're just trying to survive this interaction.

"What's in the car? You got drugs in the car? You better tell me if you got drugs in the car!"

"Sir, we're not doing anything. We're going to a movie. We are not drug dealers. We go to St. Pete High School, my name is William Packer. Sir, it's my mom's car. You can call her. I'm an upstanding citizen."

I literally said the words *upstanding citizen* like I was running for city council. Afterward my friends gave me shit for days about my choice of words.

They ran the tags, and everything came out clean. Of course. And so it was just one of the many, many, many, many, many unfortunate situations that happened to young Black kids growing up in the South.

"Get outta here," the cop growled, then added, "and don't run another stop sign." He had never mentioned me running a stop sign before. And I was pretty sure I hadn't.

"Yes, sir," I replied.

In J. Cole's "Neighbors" he raps, "Okay the neighbors think I'm selling dope," pointing out the perception many people have of young Black males. Especially those in neighborhoods (or driving cars) that some people don't perceive to "fit" the profile of young brothers. He then uses a clever double entendre: "Well, MFer, I am!" to drive home how dope his music is.

After the cops let us go, on the way to the mall, we started arguing among ourselves about how we should or shouldn't have handled the situation. After a while we let it go and even started laughing about it all. That's when Eric turned to me and, unbelievably, said, "I'm so glad they didn't find my weed."

6

Who Better Than You?

There Is No One Better Than You to Get Your Dreams Started

I know how hard the entertainment industry is to break into and how doubly hard it can be if you don't have a prominent last name, serious family money, or built-in connections. I get it. And I feel blessed every day that I'm in a position to lend a hand to those who are coming after me. The reality, though, is that the best way for me to help anyone who is trying to jump-start their life is for them to already be in a position of having accomplished something. It's much easier for me to help someone get to the next level than it is to help someone start from scratch. The fact of the matter is that *you* are the best person to kick things off for you. Especially when you are just starting out. It's amazing to get outside help if you can, but the fastest and most direct way oftentimes is to do what you can yourself. No matter the industry you are looking to make headway in, start something, develop something, build something—even if it's not the polished thing in your head. Create a prototype of where you want to end up. That's also the best way to get the attention of folks who can take you to the next level. When people ask how I got to where I am today, the true answer isn't what people want to hear: a *ton* of hard work that came along with going out and doing a lot of the heavy lifting myself.

After the on-campus premiere of our first movie, *Chocolate City,* at Florida A&M, we were desperate to find an actual movie theater willing to show it. I went to a local "second-run" theater in Tallahassee named I.C. Flicks. *{Narrator: Get it?}* Second-run theaters were these bygone, typically older, outdated movie houses that would play a movie for cheap prices after it had completed its theatrical run, right before going to home video. My job that day was to convince the manager, a pot-smoking, ponytail-rocking white dude who was quite content showing *The Rocky Horror Picture Show* twenty times a day, to give our movie a chance.

But it wasn't going so well. "I'm not showing your movie," Ponytail said, getting to the point quick. "I got a good gig going." He was content with the consumer base he had. And by *consumer base* I mean the white college kids who would get dressed in costume, drink plenty of beers, and see *Rocky Horror* over and over again. Myself and many of my peers at FAMU had never even heard of the movie, so I really didn't see what the big deal was.

"Come on, dude. Just give us a shot," I pleaded. But he didn't want to be bothered. He didn't want to ask corporate. He didn't want to ruffle feathers. He wanted to smoke his weed, show *Rocky Horror,* and be left alone with his cushy part-time job. But what he hadn't foreseen was that I was not about to let up. He kept waiting for me to take a Fortuitous No for an answer and leave his little office. Not a chance. We just kept going round and round. On one side was me being relentless: "Just give us one night, bro. How many people are watching *Rocky Horror* on a random Saturday? Sixteen? Seventeen? I know I can get twice that many people to come." On the other side was him shaking his head, pulling his ponytail, pulling his joint, and getting more and more stoned.

Finally, when his joint was just about gone, he said, "If I give you one night to show your movie, will you leave me alone?"

My smile was as wide as the Atlantic.

I'm pretty sure it went like that; honestly, by that time we were probably both high. When the night came for our showing, we had sold out every seat *in advance.* When I got to the theater there was a line out the door. It's hard to describe the feeling of excitement and accomplishment you get when people turn out in droves to support something you helped to create. That experience is one that still thrills me to this day. The theater sold out of tickets, they sold out of popcorn, they sold out of candy; it was mostly under-twenty-one college students with fake IDs, so of course they also sold out of beer. It did so well that night that the theater added multiple showings the next day, and those sold out too. I realized as I saw all these college kids watching *Chocolate City,* some for the third or fourth time, that this was *their* version of *Rocky Horror Picture Show.*

Monday morning, Ponytail called me into his office. He had a new joint and a freshly braided ponytail. "We need to talk," he said. Uh-oh. I knew this was going to happen. After that amazing weekend he was about to tell me that somebody had broken something in the theater because it was so packed and now I was going to have to pay for it.

"Your movie did so well this weekend that I want to show it next weekend and the weekend after that and the weekend after that." Oh my, how his tone had changed. *Chocolate City* ran for over a month at that theater. I imagine Ponytail is somewhere right now in the corner office of a major theater chain, balding and high. You're welcome.

My next movie was an indie called *Trois. {Narrator: It's pronounced "twah" as in ménage à trois, and it's about what you think it's about. Everybody pronounced it wrong. They should have come up with a better title.}* Think an erotic thriller in the vein of *Basic Instinct* with African American characters.

A journalist buddy gave me his press pass so I could sneak into the annual ShoWest (now called CinemaCon) theatrical exhibitors convention in Las Vegas to try and secure distribution. While there, I finagled my way into a press conference for that year's Entertainer of the Year, who happened to be a hot young movie star named Will Smith.

Now, for most people, just being in that room would have been cool enough. I wasn't even supposed to be at this convention, much less inside this press conference. But of course, me being me, I had to push the envelope even further. So I'm in this Vegas conference room with all these real journalists who *look* like journalists. Middle-aged white dudes with tape recorders and I-spend-a-lot-of-time-at-a-desk bellies. In my mind I was blending in. I had the same lanyard as everybody else. I thought I looked like a movie industry reporter. {*Narrator: Will Packer was definitely not blending in and certainly did not look like a movie industry reporter. He was twenty-four years old, one of two Black people in the room, and the other one was the famous actor onstage.*} During the Q&A everybody's raising their hand so I raise my hand. And Will Smith actually calls on me! Now, prior to this the press had been asking deep probing questions about Will's motivation as an actor, methodology for his latest role, and personal pursuits outside of the industry.

"Will Packer, *Atlanta Daily Bugle*," I said confidently, making up the name of a newspaper on the fly. I then proceeded to ask the dumbest question ever: "Mr. Smith, can you tell us about your first role?" The most inane, not-for-this-room question you might ask if you were a middle schooler writing an extra-credit paper on Will Smith. Will looked at me quizzically, but I could tell he was the kind to help out the only other young brother in the room. I recall him giving a basic courtesy answer with a little elaboration to flower it up. I said, "Thank you, Mr. Smith" as I sat down. I didn't even have a pen or a notebook to fake scribble down his answer to my fake question.

A grizzled dude next to me leaned over and said sarcastically, "You're not gonna write that down?"

"Naw, I got it," I replied as I tapped my temple. Jerk. Before he moved on, Will kind of looked at me again, like, I wonder what's up with that dude. Whatever. I was in the room, so why not? I just should've had a better question ready. I figured our paths would cross again. {Narrator: Such a poorly veiled foreshadow. Dun dun dun!}

For the rest of the convention, I did the most valuable thing you can do when you're in an unfamiliar environment. I listened. A lot. I sat in every panel I could and took notes. I learned insider lingo and exhibitor business strategies and challenges. The challenges they faced proved to be the most valuable intel. I learned that all the movie theater chains were basically in the red. They were having financial problems because, to keep up with one another, they built these giant twenty-four-theater multiplexes with stadium seating and Dolby surround sound, new technology at the time, which happened to be very expensive. And they weren't making money because they couldn't fill all those seats. A big hit movie like *Jurassic Park* was great for their industry, but they couldn't put it on all twenty-four screens.

I made sure I shook hands with all the execs from AMC, Loews, Regal, and all the major chains. Then I got the business cards of all their assistants. After the convention I dialed them up and said, "Hey, I found a dead weekend where there aren't a lot of movies. Ask your boss about giving me your smallest house to play my hot new independent movie *Trois* for one weekend? I think this could make you look really smart." I had learned the industry parlance that a house was an individual theater in a multiplex, and I knew they were looking for ways to bring in any money they could on slow weekends. Empowering the support staff with the incentive that this could make them look good was very strategic.

I got told no a lot. But I got some yeses. I was ultimately able to convince four different chains to show our movie in nineteen theaters across eighteen different markets for one weekend. These cities were all primarily in the Southeast. Then I drove to every single city. I didn't open in New York and L.A. because they were too far and too expensive. I opened in places where I knew my audience was en masse; I call them "demographic-rich" locations. I went from Atlanta to Jackson, Mississippi; to Birmingham, Alabama; to Greensboro, North Carolina; to Raleigh, to Memphis, to Jacksonville, and so on. I can tell you every city, because I literally drove to every one. Every. Single. One.

Most cities it was just my partner Rob Hardy and me, and we would stay at the cheapest hotel we could find. Then we would go to the local radio station and beg someone in charge to give us sixty seconds of airtime to promote our movie release in that city. Then we would go to the local churches *and* the local nightclubs and blanket cars in the parking lots with our promotional flyers. Same flyers for both venues, in case you were wondering. And a lot of times it was the same cars parked in front of both venues. I mean, this is the South after all.

Our grassroots efforts paid off. We opened in our nineteen theaters to the highest per-screen average in the country. Soon other theaters in other cities started calling and saying, "Hey, bring that movie to us. We'll play it."

We got calls from theaters in Texas. Theaters in Michigan. Theaters in Oakland. I remember saying there is no way we could ever open in Oakland because that's just too far to drive. The theater owner said, "You know, you don't have to come yourself. Nobody does that. Just ship us a print of the movie like everybody else does." I still laugh thinking about how that legitimately had not occurred to us at that point.

Here's the thing: The only reason I have the stature to write a book that you care enough to read is because I convinced those first theater chains to give me their smallest house on a slow weekend. Then, by driving to each and every city and doing whatever it took to generate excitement, we were able to pack the one theater we had in that town. We ultimately made just over $1 million at the box office on our own without major distribution. That, my friends, got people in Hollywood talking.

If you want to get the attention of Hollywood, make money without them. I remember getting a call from someone at Sony Pictures while I was at the worldwide corporate headquarters of our film company (which was the third bedroom of the three-bedroom house we were renting in an Atlanta suburb), who mispronounced the name of the movie. Looking back, although it felt clever to call a movie about a *ménage à trois* gone wrong the French word for "three," I now realize we could've had a better title because nobody knew how to say it. *{Narrator: Told you.}* When the call came in from Sony Pictures looking for the producer of *Troyce,* I said, "Please hold." Then I screamed out loud, "Sony is on the phone!"

Rob ran into the room.

"So, what are you gonna say?"

"I have no idea," I replied.

I then proceeded to tell them that they were looking for Will Packer but he was in meetings all morning and I'd have to take a message. Yep, always had healthy arrogance. I knew Hollywood was all about perception, so I decided to create this perception of an extremely busy executive who had this hot movie and lots and lots of meetings. Meanwhile, I was in my spare bedroom in boxer shorts, eating ramen noodles and taking calls on a ten-dollar cordless phone with a broken antenna.

Sony ended up doing a deal with us for the home video distribution of *Trois.* Hollywood called after we started making money on our own. Getting to that point was tough. There were many long, lonely nights driving through small towns, staying in bad hotels, and getting told, "Get outta my face!" over and over while trying to get people to support our movie. But that's what it took. That Sony deal kick-started my Hollywood movie career, but we had to put in the work on our own to get there. This may look different if the industry you are looking to crack isn't Hollywood, but the playbook is the same: Make yourself valuable to said industry. And do that not by waiting on someone else to assist you. Do that by using the resources you currently have at hand, the most valuable of which, by far, is *you*.

ALWAYS BE A DOER, NOT A TALKER

I got a great piece of advice from pioneering filmmaker Warrington Hudlin. Right after college, I was interning on the set of his movie *Ride*, and I badly wanted him to watch *Chocolate City*. When there was a break between scenes, I approached him and began to tell him my story as a young aspiring filmmaker. I could see his eyes starting to glaze over at yet another filmmaker pitching him, until I pulled out a freshly shrink-wrapped VHS copy of my film. Once he saw the packaging he stopped me, looked me right in the eyes, and said, "Young brother, *this* is what separates you from most people in Hollywood. I have no idea whether this movie is good or bad. It's probably bad, but honestly, not the point. The fact that you have a finished product in an industry where everyone is talking about what they're *going* to do, what they're *about* to do, and what they're *planning* to do: This distinguishes you. You've actually *done* something. Always be a *doer*, not a talker."

One of my personal mottoes is "It's the work you put in when nobody's watching that makes everybody pay attention later." People are always talking instead of putting the work in. Social media has given everyone their own personal platform. I think largely that's a good thing. But by definition the value of these individual platforms is diminished because *everyone* has one. A lot of people like to talk just because they can. Some do it for attention or likes, or to be agitators for agitation's sake. Far fewer are doing it toward an actual goal. Go put your head down and start actually working toward something. Let everybody else talk. Then guess what happens? When you come up for air, what do you think they're going to be talking about? You and the work you put in.

I'm blessed to work in an industry that is driven by ideas. I get pitched ideas all the time. Some good, most awful. But it's not just about having an idea; it's about actually doing the legwork to make it happen. As the Bible says, faith without works is dead.

An idea is just that. A thought. It doesn't unlock its real value until it's acted on. An amazing idea is like going out and finding the perfect pair of running shoes as you stand at the starting line of a marathon. They're laced up tight. They fit perfect. You're raring to go. But whether you're successful or not depends on what happens after the starting gun goes off. Yes, you need those perfect shoes with the right cushion, the right balance, and the right weight. But the real work is in the 26.2 miles that lie ahead of you. Never forget that.

You can prepare all you want, but until you actually begin your journey you don't truly know how ready you are to tackle the challenges ahead. When facing major decisions, we often seek certainty and detailed plans before we take the leap. We want everything to be perfectly aligned, every question answered, and that can paralyze us and make us frozen with indecision. I got a great piece of advice from Richard Lovett, head of the famed Hollywood talent agency Creative Artists Agency. He told me, "Sometimes you just have to start climbing the mountain." He explained how the unknowns reveal themselves as you embark on a journey. There will always be uncertainties, unforeseen obstacles that arise along the way. The true test lies in our ability to adapt, adjust, and keep climbing. It was a powerful analogy that resonated deeply with me.

So, to anyone standing at the foot of their own metaphorical mountain, I say this: Don't talk about it, *be* about it. And don't wait to have all the answers before you begin. Trust in your preparation, gather your courage, and take that first step. Embrace the unknowns, adapt as you go, and let the journey reveal the path forward. As you climb, you'll discover the resilience within you and reach new heights you never thought possible.

7

The Enemy Is to the North

Find Your Rock

I've produced in many genres: ensemble comedies, thrillers, docs, rom-coms, but personally I'm also a big fan of sci-fi and fantasy. Growing up I was into Dungeons & Dragons–style games and books. Some might say "nerd," but I prefer "fantasy content aficionado." In fact, one of my favorite shows is *Game of Thrones.* The world creation, sorcery, and dragons are right up my alley.

One of my favorite concepts within the show is how, when all these various kingdoms were warring with one another, there was this *huge* unbeatable army of undead zombie types coming to destroy them all from the north. The more prescient characters in the show were repeatedly screaming, "Yo! Chill, y'all! We can't be fighting among ourselves! All this conflict is irrelevant, fam! The true enemy is to the north!" *{Narrator: Yeah, something like that.}*

My wife Heather and I have adopted this mantra in our marriage. Whenever we're bickering about something that feels major at the time but is really trivial in the scheme of things, one of us will just remind the other, "Baby, the enemy is to the north." The implication is that although we may be heated and angry in this moment, we need to step back and realize the true enemy is not either of us. Most often it's some external factor that we may or may not have control over. Instead of directing the anger and negativity toward each other, let's put it toward trying to vanquish the *real* enemy.

It's really, really hard to be great. It's even harder by yourself or when you're in a bad relationship. As humans we're not built to be by ourselves. We're made to be communal. Even if you think you're the ultimate introvert, please understand that you still *need* other people to attain any substantive level of success. You just can't do it all alone.

That said, there's nothing more draining, more time-consuming, and more detrimental to one's goals (personal *and* career) than a bad romantic relationship. Being in an awful romance is *the worst*. You spend so much physical and emotional energy dealing with the negativity that there is no way you can perform at your highest levels in any other aspect of your life. It's like being in a sailboat race with a leaky boat. You're so focused on keeping the water out of the hull that you're not adjusting the sails and maneuvering like you should.

Conversely, a positive, healthy, supportive relationship can lift your non-romantic endeavors in ways that can't be overstated. Now, we all know loving someone is important, feeling loved is amazing validation, and so on. That's not what I'm focused on. I love my wife to death. Can't imagine living without her. This next statement may be controversial, but the reality is that finding and nurturing a relationship with Heather was an amazing *business* decision for me as well. She hates when I say that out loud, even though she knows it's true. I tell her, "Baby, you make my life worth living. You make me better in every way. My emotional head and my business head see the value in that. You get what I'm saying, right?"

"I'm still processing," she'll say.

I derive strength and confidence from my marriage, from the fact that I have somebody who I feel like, no matter what, has my back, 100 percent. That strength and confidence spills over into career endeavors. I walk into a business meeting feeling like I'm the greatest person in that room because someone I love and respect has literally told me that earlier that day. The person on the other side of the table who's had their self-esteem eroded by negativity from their significant other doesn't stand a chance. Once I realized that Heather was the one who would light up my life, make my days better and my life worth living, the pragmatist in me knew I needed to *lock that down.* I proposed to her in front of sixty thousand people onstage at the Essence Festival of Culture in New Orleans. I like to say that I needed to put public pressure on her to say yes. I'm joking . . . mostly. I mean, I was pretty sure at that point she was saying yes, but why take chances?

Another show Heather and I are fans of is *The Crown.* Now, I personally think the whole setup of the monarchy and royal family is batshit crazy. I can't even imagine being subjected to all the rigidness, pomp, circumstance, and public scrutiny of that life. However, there is something about the royal family that Heather and I emulate. They are *committed* to that life. With very few exceptions, once you're in that world either by birth or marriage you are in it—for life. Most marriage vows reference better or worse. The monarchy takes it to another level. Historically, leaving just wasn't an option for them. *{Narrator: Well, until Harry and Meghan flipped all the palace tables over and said, "We out!"}*

When you're in a situation and leaving is not an option, you find ways to make the best of the circumstances you're faced with. Most times you do exactly that and the situation improves if you're willing to work at it. Conversely, if leaving a situation is an option, then when things get uncomfortable that option starts to look appealing. Inevitably, at some point you're probably going to choose the option to get out if it exists.

This is true of any bad situation, but we apply it to our marriage. Honestly, Heather deserves all the credit for instilling that mentality. I like to say I've been trying to leave her for years but she won't let me, and Heather likes to say, "You ain't going *nowhere*." I say it jokingly. She does not. Either way, our mindset: We're in it forever.

See, there *is* something good to come from the monarchy. It almost makes up for the fact that they colonized and oppressed people for trillions of years, right?

So, yes, I love my wife immeasurably. Yes, she makes me happy beyond words. Also, I'm a driven, highly ambitious businessperson and I realize that I am made better by having someone who's constantly in my corner and I can count on, who's always supporting me and pushing me to be my best self. If you have somebody who boosts your drive to be successful, a rock that when everything is going wrong in business you know has your back no matter what—when you walk into any meeting, any room, any challenge, you will do so with a different level of confidence. It could be romantic, it could be a best friend, it could be a family member lifting you up. Either way, that support will help you unlock your greatest potential. But if it *is* a romantic partner, at least you'll have someone to keep you warm when the undead zombie army gets to town.

HEATHER BE LYING

My wife Heather sounds pretty great, doesn't she? She's not. She ain't that great. I'll tell you why.

A few years back, Heather and I were on vacation in Saint Bart's with another couple, Janora and Leila. The trip was amazing. We were there during off-peak season so it wasn't very crowded and the weather was perfect. One day we were all snorkeling near some beautiful reefs just off the coast of a secluded beach area. The colors in the water were amazing and we were the only ones out there, so it made for a very tranquil scene. As I was exploring some vibrant bright-red coral, I thought I heard my name. I could see Janora and Leila snorkeling a few feet away to my right. I looked around for Heather but didn't see her, which was odd because I could have sworn she was right next to me. I came up to the surface and saw her about thirty feet away, swimming toward the shore.

"Babe!" I yelled. "Is something wrong?"

This is where it got weird. Without breaking her stroke she yelled back at me, "Come on!"

Now she was halfway to the shore. She didn't really look like she was panic-swimming and she was far enough away that I couldn't tell if I detected real alarm in her voice or not.

"Did something happen?" I yelled. "Should I get Janora and Leila?"

This time she looked back at me as she was continuing to swim away and I would describe the look on her face as serious. She didn't appear to be terrified, but she also wasn't laughing and smiling like we all had been. She took a beat like she was considering my question, and again, without stopping, said "Probably" and continued to swim.

Okay, now I was like WTF. So I immediately yelled for Leila, who was the closest to me. She came to the surface.

"What's up?"

"Hey. Heather says we need to come to shore."

"What happened?"

"I have no idea."

"Well, should I get Janora?"

"Definitely." Now I started to swim with a purpose. When I looked up, what I saw made no sense. Heather, now on the shore, was standing on the beach holding a flimsy foam water toy. She had it outstretched toward me and was yelling, with urgency this time, "Come on! Grab this!"

What?

It looked absurd. It wasn't like there was some steep drop-off into the water, yet she was standing on the sand telling me to grab a pink pool noodle. She was acting as if the water itself was poisonous or something.

Something clearly was wrong. Heart racing, arms pumping, and legs kicking, I swam to the shore as fast as I could. I could hear Janora and Leila swimming behind me. They were yelling, "Heather, what's wrong?" But she wasn't answering.

When I finally made it to shore after what seemed like forever, I was breathless.

"Baby, what's wrong?!"

She finally started talking. "There's a shark!"

"What? Where?! What kind?"

"A tiger shark!"

My eyes widened. Now, Heather and I are by no means shark experts, but we probably know more about sharks than the average person. This is due to the fact that I've had the opportunity to produce the opening night of the Discovery Channel's Shark Week multiple times. I've learned a lot getting a chance to work with some of the top marine biologists and shark experts in the world, and I've shared a lot of that knowledge with Heather. She knows exactly what a tiger shark looks like. And I know that a tiger shark is the second most aggressive shark of them all. Right behind great whites. I also know that a tiger shark is what they term a nonselective predator. That basically means that a tiger shark will eat whatever's around. They've found everything from license plates to fur coats in the stomachs of tiger sharks. Not only will a tiger shark eat your face, it'll eat your bike too.

Now I panic and start yelling to Janora and Leila, "Tiger shark! Come on! Get out of the water!"

As they start really booking it to shore, I turned to Heather. "Why didn't you tell me that?"

"I didn't want you to panic," she said.

I was thinking, "Didn't want me to panic?" Sometimes there's a time to panic. Getting out of the water when there's a tiger shark around feels like one of those good moments to panic. *[Narrator: Don't listen to Will. If you are in the water and see a tiger shark, or any shark for that matter, don't panic. Leave the water quickly and calmly.]* Thankfully Janora and Leila made it to shore and the four of us were able to find a vantage point from some jutting rocks off the beach and look down near the reef where we just were. Sure enough, there was about a twelve-foot tiger shark cruising the reef, minding its business.

It was right at that exact moment that it occurred to me what had *actually* happened.

Now, understand that Heather and I are very lovey-dovey and affirmational in the way we talk to each other. We're one of those couples that make other couples sick with a bunch of "I love you more than life itself," "I would give up my right arm for you," "I could never live without you" kind of talk. In fact, Heather herself has said with real conviction, "I would jump in front of a train for you!" I personally can't think of a single real-life scenario where that specific self-sacrificing act would ever be necessary, and I make movies for a living! But no matter, it feels amazing when she says it.

I now know that all that is complete and utter equine feces.

Heather will say I'm exaggerating about what happened in Saint Bart's. Don't listen to her. I am not. I know what happened—Heather saw that tiger shark while we were all swimming and got understandably shook. She then made a very specific calculation. She figured there are four people in the water and one tiger shark. I imagine the conversation she had in her head: "There's no way that I can outswim this shark. But if I very carefully start making my way to shore, then I can be sure to outswim the other three people in the water. If the shark realizes at some point that there are tasty humans nearby, I will have a much better chance of survival if he has started to munch on the others first. I love my husband, and I would prefer he not become shark brunch, so once I'm halfway to safety I'll alert him so he can try to get away. If by chance I don't make it and the shark does get to me, by then he will be so full of Janora, Leila, and if necessary Will, that hopefully he won't want any Heather."

I explained my theory later that night at dinner when we were all safe and sound. "That's not what happened!" Heather protested. "I told you to come on and get out of the water."

"Yeah, after you were already halfway to the beach," I said. "How else were you out of the water way before me?"

"I'm just a faster swimmer than you, that's all."

"Heather, are you saying that when we were snorkeling next to each other and you saw the shark that you told me right then?" I asked.

"Who wants more wine?" she said.

Here's the thing: Self-preservation is the most basic human instinct. I get that. My son Zion is a certified lifeguard, and they are taught that somebody who thinks they're drowning will literally kill you trying to save themselves. They cannot help it. They think they're dying. And they will grab on to anything. They tell you as a lifeguard to grab a person from behind to make sure that you've got a grip on them and they can't grab hold of you because they will unintentionally pull you under the water to save themselves. You have to make sure you are secure.

It's something we all have to do, even in non-life-threatening situations. Take care of ourselves first. The classic "put your oxygen mask on before you try to help somebody else." Taking care of yourself first isn't about being selfish; it's about self-care. On top of that, you can't help anyone at all if you're a mess. I tell my employees all the time, "Hey, if things aren't right at home, if you have something that's seriously hindering you personally, like mental health, you can't deliver for this company. If you need time, you come to me and you let me know. Make taking care of yourself the priority. I'll never ask you to put this company first. Put yourself first, because I know that when things are right with you, you are then able to give your best to the company."

In hindsight, without emotion attached, I realize my wife's self-preservation instinct kicked in. It sounds wildly romantic to say you'd sacrifice your own life for someone else, but that's something we make look glamorous in the movies. That ain't real life, buddy. Heather wasn't trying to kill me or purposely have me get eaten by a shark, and I know she does care about my well-being. Just not more than hers. That's pretty human, I suppose.

Janora and Leila forgave Heather and laughed about it that night. Me? I'm still processing.

8

Take the Thunder Out

Learn to Be a Professional Defuser

Hollywood is an industry driven by creativity with a lot of huge egos and people who take everything extremely seriously. I kid you not, one time an agent sobbed real tears on the phone with me because her client wasn't going to get extra tickets to a movie premiere. That wasn't the first or last time I dealt with full-on weeping or in some instances top-of-lungs screaming. Crises happen 24/7 in Hollywood. Some actual, some perceived, but all very real to the folks involved. For all the amazing moments of achievement and joy that I love, Tinseltown can also be the land of venom and backstabbing. All the pressure, money, power, and fame gets to people. There are a lot of people in my industry who are angry and unhappy all the time.

In my role as producer, I defuse explosive situations on an almost daily basis. I'm constantly putting out fires. From keeping it cool on the Las Vegas set of *Think Like a Man Too,* where scorching summer temps were literally one hundred–plus degrees and at times the relations between the studio and filmmaking team were even hotter, to handling an actual blaze on a movie set when candles an actor kept lit to hide the smell of marijuana they would partake in between scenes got knocked over and the trailer caught fire, and one of the other actors swore it was all *my* fault.

Oh, and there was that one A-list star who kept showing up to set late and intoxicated, pissing off an entire cast and crew. I've had to deal with fistfights and clandestine on-set romances that went bad between actors who then had to work together for many more weeks. I once even had to forcibly enter the hotel room of an actor who had been unresponsive for hours after his call time. We thought he was dead. He was not. He was butt naked and severely hungover. When he saw me in the room, he had no idea who I was. He tried to kiss me. I said, "First of all, we're not doing that. Second of all, put some clothes on. It's time to get your ass to work. Third of all, refer back to first of all." Can't make this stuff up.

Through all that drama, I've learned that the best way to weather the storm is to take the thunder out. Let me tell you what I mean. You'd never know by the phenomenal end product, but the first day of shooting my ensemble action movie *Takers* was a disaster. We had a dope all-star cast—Paul Walker (RIP), Idris Elba, Hayden Christensen, Michael Ealy, Zoe Saldana, T.I., Chris Brown—but the whole darn thing almost fell apart over Paul Walker's hair and wardrobe.

Paul was kind of a hippie. He would just as soon be chilling on a beach in Hawaii as sitting in a hair-and-makeup trailer on a movie set. So it wasn't terribly surprising when on the first day of production he rolled onto set with long dirty-blond hair, a scruffy beard, ripped jeans, and a T-shirt. Now, our filmmaking team, including the movie studio, had a different idea about the cast's aesthetic. It was an action movie about a slick crew of thieves who pulled off sophisticated heists. We had a great-looking cast. We wanted these handsome guys in tailored suits with clean cuts. We wanted to play beyond the typical action audience, which is young males, so our goal was to also get women's butts in those movie theater seats.

We wanted them in suits and ties; Paul wanted to wear ripped jeans and baseball hats. That was how he believed he looked his most hip and "sexiest." So that's how he showed up to set. Now, that was no big deal. I've had actors show up looking all kinds of crazy before the professional glam squad gets their hands on them. The difference was that Paul wasn't interested in changing his look much. He liked his look. He thought it was cool—and make no mistake, it was, just not for the character.

My guy Clint Culpepper, who ran the division of Sony that was financing the movie, started arguing with Paul right away. He objected, "No, no, no. Anybody on the street can look like that. You guys have to look different. You have to look straight out of *GQ* magazine."

Paul was not having it. He kept pushing back and got increasingly irate. It very quickly escalated into a heated argument outside of the hair-and-makeup trailer. Clint is a passionate executive who is known for being a yeller and a screamer at times. This was one of those times. Paul was much more mild-mannered, but Clint's approach was bringing out the fire in him and he was not backing down. "This is not what I signed up for," Paul fumed. "I'm not doing that. [Bleep] this. I'm not doing this movie." And he stormed off back to his trailer and slammed the door.

Now at this point, I've got cameras set up; I've got all my other actors coming out of makeup, ready to go; I've got the studio exec mad at one of my star actors; and I've got said star actor saying he was about to catch the next flight back to Hawaii. Every minute of their argument was causing a delay, which equaled cold hard cash flushing down the drain. One of the chief concerns of a movie producer is to bring the production in on time and on budget.

The first assistant director, who is charged with running the set, turned to me and said, "What are we going to do?" I knew I didn't want my other actors to hear about it because then it would become an even bigger thing. I had quietly gotten the same pushback from Idris Elba around the look of the cast for the film. But because I knew Idris well and we had worked together before, we hashed it out behind closed doors before it spilled over publicly on set. He had begrudgingly agreed to do the clean-cut, suit look. But I knew if he and the other actors got wind of Paul's adamant pushback, I could have a full-blown revolt on my hands. I formulated a plan. I told the director, John Luessenhop, "Shoot what you can without Paul and make it seem like this is what you always intended. Don't make it a big deal that Paul's not on set."

I knocked on Paul's trailer. I heard a gruff "Yeah" from the other side of the door. When I walked in, I could tell Paul was still on a hundred. He was heated and was ready for whatever lame argument he thought I might come with about why our vision for the movie was right. I came in and I didn't even sit down. The very first thing I said was "I am so sorry." Then I underscored the sincerity of my apology. Not because he was right and the other guy was wrong. Not because he was wrong and the other guy was right. Because I had to take the thunder out.

I started, "I'm really sorry that on the first day of this movie, our first time working together, you are so unhappy and that this experience has been so negative to this point." Then I apologized again. "I'm sincerely sorry, man. I take a lot of pride in putting my talent in position to succeed. It doesn't even matter how we got here. We are here. And I want you to hear that from me. I apologize. I thought the plan for the movie look had been communicated, but apparently that wasn't done clearly enough, and that's on me. I take it personally, and I'm going to make it my mission to make sure that every day from this point forward is better than today. Because on a Will Packer set, I never want you to feel the way you're feeling right now. I take full responsibility for that." I said it and I meant it.

My approach did two crucial things. Number one, it shifted the blame to me. It gave Paul somebody that he could tangibly assign fault to who wasn't this exec that he was having a major problem with. I was expendable in this scenario. The other thing it did was show Paul somebody felt remorse for him being upset and told him that it's going to be better from this point forward. I'll never forget what Paul said next. He took a deep breath, was quiet for a few moments, and then:

"I get it. You're the good cop. But you're a damn good one. I feel you. Will, I know it's not about you, and I'm going to figure it out. We're going to make it work, and we'll move forward."

Paul was still upset, but the crisis was over. Situation de-escalated. Achievement unlocked. When you go see the movie, you see a clean-cut, clean-shaven Paul Walker wearing suits. You see Idris Elba and all the guys wearing dinner jackets, pocket squares, ties, and cuff links. Everybody was super fly. After the fact, every single actor talked about how much they liked the look and how that was the right call for the movie. They looked good. They were getting complimented for it. Audiences liked how they looked. So Clint ultimately was right, but on day one it was a very precarious situation. *Takers* was *thisclose* to going down in flames.

When I have cast or co-workers arguing, my philosophy is, look past the usual thinking of one side having an idea of what the solution should be and the other side having a counter perspective to that approach. I'm always thinking about a solution that will ultimately be the best result for the team or project. When I have a difficult actor, for example, I look at the elements that are making this person difficult and figure out which of those elements I can remove and at what cost. If the cost is worth it, then I do it. Without regard to my own emotions or feelings. I do what makes sense. Period. Then I make it my mission to make sure that every day from this point forward is better than today. That ensures you don't end up dealing with the same conflict twice.

On *Takers* I took the blame because someone had to. Ego had to be moved out of the way to move things forward. There was a time when a high-profile actor friend of mine who shall remain nameless . . . *{Narrator: We're not doing that in this book, Will. Just tell the people it was Idris Elba.}* Okay fine, it was Idris. Idris was nominated for an Outstanding Lead Actor Emmy for the first time ever. He was being dressed by a very high-profile designer, but just two hours before the show he called said designer to say the outfit was ill-fitting and had a giant stain on it. He was angry and disappointed. He refused to walk the red carpet, and I don't blame him. He was apoplectic and ready to chop heads off.

But then a senior rep for the designer took charge. She rushed over to his hotel suite with a whole stylist crew in tow as a show of force to help him get ready at lightning speed. The first thing she did when she waltzed in carrying a fresh new suit was say, "We messed up, this is on us, you shouldn't be in this situation, we should have had a backup suit, and we are going to fix this. Get up. It's time to get dressed. We have thirty minutes to get you to the carpet. Let's go."

"Well, wait a minute, what happened with the other suit?! Somebody messed up . . ." he started.

"We don't have time for that right now. This is our fault but now we're gonna get you to that show. Take your pants off." *{Narrator: How many ladies would love to say that to Mr. Elba?}*

He indeed did take his pants off, put on the backup suit, they altered it on the spot to fit him perfectly, and he made it to the show on time, looking sharp as always. Turns out, it was actually *his* fault because he had taken the original suit to get pressed at the dry cleaner, which had ironed the stain onto the suit, because they didn't know how to handle really fine Italian fabric. But that detail came out later, and it didn't really matter at that point. The rep didn't come in with, "This isn't our fault." She came in with, "It's all my fault. I'm gonna fix it, but I gotta move now in order to fix it. This is what we do. We fix our mistakes. We effed up. I'm not going to let you go out there like that. I'm not going to let you possibly win your first Emmy looking like a fool." That's right, she took the thunder out.

If she had done it the other way and tried to argue back and forth about what happened, he would've missed the show completely. Because, believe me, he was understandably ready to argue the point that it was this big designer's fault that he was left high and dry. She removed the possibility of a long drawn-out time-consuming argument by taking blame and apologizing for "our horrific mistake." Adding a zesty little adjective like *horrific* was a boss move too. A "my bad" goes a long way with angry people.

Trust me, taking the thunder out works on everyone, even me. One time I had to do a promo video for the Oprah Winfrey Network with my family during the Covid pandemic days. This was when everybody was shooting cellphone videos at home while we all sheltered in place. Many major networks would air these videos because it was the only access they could get to run fresh content. The concept was Oprah from her home showcasing all her talent and producers from their homes with their families letting everybody know we would all get through this time together. I alerted the Six-Pack that I would need them. When the time came, none of my kids showed up. I texted, COME ON, GUYS, IT'S TIME TO DO THE SHOOT. Nobody took it seriously and nobody responded to me. They didn't care; they were all in their rooms playing video games. I was so angry. And it hurt, if I'm being honest.

Heather was like, "I'll go get them."

And I said, "You know what? Don't bother. I asked them to be here. I told them it was important to me. Nobody showed up. That tells me all I need to know. Leave them where they are." I did the video with just Heather, and I vowed to tear into their little privileged spoiled asses at a dinner we were having the next night. I was going to let these kids have it.

But a crazy thing happened. The next day, the kids each gave me heartfelt, old-school cards with handwritten apologies. "I messed up," they wrote. "This was important to you. I'm so sorry." The apologies felt so sincere, so real, it totally took the thunder out of me.

One thing about angry people who feel they are in the right is that they are just waiting for the opportunity to tell you, me, the offending party, and the whole world how right they are. That was Paul, that was Idris, and that was me. But oftentimes if you admit your part from the door, even if you don't have to, even if you think you're not *that* wrong . . . you can get past the conflict.

If you're honest and truly remorseful in important relationships, you can get somebody to move past their anger or resentment to the point of focusing on what's really important. Be it something you're trying to accomplish or the relationship itself. Sometimes people actually *want* to be angry all the time. It's easy to stay mad. It can feel good to say "I'm right and you're wrong." But if you're both yelling that at the top of your lungs, nothing is getting accomplished. Never underestimate the power of an apology. A coward is somebody who's afraid to say "I'm sorry." Don't be a coward. Stand up. Say it. Be definitive and own your mistakes. It does multiple things: It gives you power, and it gives you leverage. Once the apology is there, you can move past it.

If you are someone who needs to hear this—hear this: Apologies aren't weak; they make you stronger. And they allow you to move forward with strength.

Triumph and Disaster

Reject Both the Romanticization of Perfection and the Absoluteness of Failure

Rudyard Kipling wrote a lot of poems. Like *a lot.* Over five hundred. With that expansive a catalog, I would imagine he has some hits and some misses. I don't claim to be a Kipling authority, but one thing I know for sure is that my man Rudyard has one particular work in his arsenal that is a certified, indisputable, A-one banger. If you haven't guessed it, I'm talking about "If—," his quintessential masterpiece. I had the privilege of committing the entire poem to memory when I was a sophomore at Florida A&M pledging the Alpha Phi Alpha fraternity. By *privilege* I mean that my life depended on me learning that poem forward and backward. The line that always stood out to me the most is "If you can meet with triumph and disaster / And treat those two impostors just the same." I wholeheartedly subscribe to the notion that Rudyard Kipling puts forth: that both triumph and disaster are impostors. Neither of them is genuine.

I reject the extremes of perfection and abject failure. The reality is that while you may not be that great, you ain't that awful either. Give the ideas of unblemished flawlessness and utter calamity both the same value. Treat those two impostors just the same. They're both just constructs of flawed human minds that badly need validation. You don't have the nearly thirty-year career I have had in the movie industry without having a bunch of triumphs and a bunch of disasters. The reason I have sustained has less to do with the highs of my victories or the lows of my defeats and more to do with my ability to keep an even keel through it all. Robert De Niro has a great quote: "When things are going well, just be calm."

I mentioned that I pledged Alpha Phi Alpha. I should probably give that some context. Black Greek letter organizations are hundred-year-old pillars within the Black community. They were formed to uplift and create a sense of belonging for Black college students who were denied admittance into white organizations. Oftentimes fathers and mothers pass on eye color, personality traits, and a respect and appreciation for a particular fraternity or sorority. Alpha Phi Alpha is the oldest of the Black Greek orgs. My father was an Alpha man. He instilled in me a love and admiration for the first African American Greek letter organization from birth. He made it clear when I left for college that I *did not* have to pledge Alpha but that I *could not* pledge any other fraternity. Not if I wanted to come home.

When I finally got the opportunity to cross the burning sands of Alpha in the spring of 1993, it was a life-defining moment for me. It was the first time I remember feeling pure unadulterated pride about something that I had done "on my own" without my parents. I say "on my own," but I really never was. I pledged with eighteen other line brothers who I'm still very close with to this day. I became an Alpha man. The same fraternity as the great Reverend Dr. Martin Luther King, Jr., and so many other esteemed Alphas. I loved Alpha then, and I love Alpha now.

Triumph.

When I made *Stomp the Yard,* I always intended it as a love letter to Black Greek life and HBCUs disguised as a dance movie. During the production process, I was painstaking about making sure that while the lead characters and fraternities were fictional, I included very accurate depictions of real Black Greeks in the film. I reached out and included local fraternity and sorority chapter members to populate the film and give it authenticity. People on the production would comment about the lengths I was going to to ensure these portrayals were accurate and respectful. I made sure only actual Greek members wore the letters and symbols, never just background actors who were not affiliated. Before they performed the first dance number, I made sure all my actors understood that their portrayals were based on real-life organizations with rich histories and legacies. And it wasn't just about my beloved Alphas. I made sure that every single Black Greek letter organization was depicted in some way in the movie. I even reached out to the national offices of all the frats and sororities. I wanted to let them know what I was doing. I didn't need anything per se, but I wanted them to know that a movie was being made by one of their own and I would appreciate any support they could lend when it was time to promote the movie.

I thought it slightly strange when not one of the national bodies responded to me. But I chalked it up to them not really having time to respond. Plus, I was very busy making a movie, so I didn't have time to dwell on it. When the movie was completed I knew I had something special. Not only was the stepping in the movie top-notch but I was also proud of our depiction of Black Greek life. Now, when you are in post-production on a film, it's typical for the movie studio's legal team to go through an intensive process of *t* crossing and *i* dotting. They review every contract and watch the film forward and backward to ensure there is nothing in it that could be legally problematic. Big Hollywood movies attract a lot of attention, and not all of it is well-intentioned. There is a whole bottom-feeder industry of people who try to make money off suing movie studios.

During post-production on *Stomp the Yard,* I got a call from one of the studio attorneys asking if we had gotten releases from the real fraternities and sororities we portrayed in the film. "Did I need to?" I asked. I had gone through a pretty intensive process of legal clearances during production, and this had never come up before.

"Not particularly," I was told. "You're not portraying them in a negative context, so you have the right to show the letters and symbols. It would just be nice to have a sign-off from them if you can."

"Not a problem!" I responded. Now that we were getting ready to gear up for the release of the movie, I needed to reach back out to the national organizations anyway. I wanted them to be as involved as possible with marketing, and since I hadn't heard back from them I figured it gave me an excuse to reach out again.

Suffice to say, it didn't go like I anticipated. I called each of the national orgs again with the intent to ask them to sign waivers and to discuss marketing of the film. This time around I actually got a few of them on the phone. I'll be totally honest with you, the response was humbling. No one took me seriously. Now, I wasn't Will Packer on the level I am today with a bunch of hit movies under my belt. In fact, the biggest movie from a box-office perspective I had made to that point was the faith-based indie production *The Gospel,* which made some noise but wasn't a box-office smash by most standards. The officers of the frats and sororities that I *was* able to get on the phone seemed to barely listen to what I was saying. I would tell them about my movie and my desire to elevate the perception of Black frats and sororities and that I'd like them to authorize me using them in the movie. I would get, with a literal yawn, "Yeah, okay. Send me what ya got and we'll get back to you."

My own fraternity was no different. I sent the release to the few that asked for it. Not one followed up. I reached back out and not one took my call. Now I went from being disappointed to downright irked. Like, seriously? Y'all are gonna do me like this? *Me?* I'm trying to showcase *us.* This is a major opportunity! They didn't care. I went back to Sony Pictures and said, "Yeah, so the process of getting releases is going a little slow. . . . Can we move forward without them?"

Sony agreed to move forward once I assured them that there was no issue other than nonresponsiveness. So we plowed ahead toward our opening date. I was so focused on the marketing, promotion, and distribution of my first major studio release that I frankly forgot about the snub. Then a funny thing happened once the commercials and ads for the movie started to run. There was a buzz among the Black Greek community that there was a Hollywood movie coming out that showcased HBCUs and Greek life. This was now a big deal. It was at this moment that I got a call from the president of the movie studio, and he said that Sony had been contacted by one of the fraternities. I smiled. "I bet they did. Now that the movie is getting buzz they want to be a part of it. Which frat reached out?" I asked.

"The Alphas," he said.

"Even better. I wish they had reached out to me first, but it's all good."

"Not really. . . . They are demanding that we not release the movie and are threatening to sue if we do."

Disaster.

Once I picked my jaw up off the floor and got past the pure shock of what he'd said, I realized what was happening. The current administration of Alpha Phi Alpha . . . *my* Alpha Phi Alpha . . . had seen the promotion for *Stomp the Yard.* It looked glossy. It looked Hollywood. It looked *expensive.* They wanted to get *paid.* The Alphas created a coalition of the other Greek letter organizations and issued a cease and desist to Sony *on behalf* of all the Greek letter organizations, saying that they were uncomfortable with the portrayal of their orgs in the movie and hadn't agreed to said depictions. Of course their concerns could be allayed with a nice healthy donation.

It was easily one of the lowest moments of my professional career. I took it *personally.* How could I not? These were *my* people. *My brothers.* This was my first big movie and they were threatening to sabotage it. I got the leadership and legal representatives of the Alphas on the phone.

"How could you say you don't like the portrayal when you haven't even seen the movie?" I asked.

"We don't have to. We can tell by the trailer. It's just a bunch of stepping. We do more than that."

"Of course you do more than that. I know. I'm a member, remember. The movie is a love letter to Black Greek life."

"You should've reached out to us when you were making the movie, brother, and maybe this could have been avoided."

I can't make this up. The nerve. The disrespect. Needless to say, the call didn't go well. Fortunately for all involved, that call is not where the story ends. Large corporations don't like public disputes. Oftentimes they will pay just to make them go away. And plenty of people will try to take advantage of this fact. The Alpha administration put out a press release announcing their intention to boycott *Stomp the Yard.* This did two things: One, it made the dispute public and extremely annoying for Sony. Two, if I thought I had buzz before, this kicked it into overdrive. One way to get attention for something is to boycott it. It's like yelling, "Hey, everybody! Whatever you do, don't look over there!" Yeah, right. All of a sudden people who had never heard of *Stomp the Yard* were talking about it and asking when it would be released.

This very unfortunate controversy had an unexpected outcome. First, I decided, although I didn't have to, to digitally remove all the Greek letters and symbols of the actual fraternities and sororities from *Stomp the Yard.* That is why if you watch the movie today you only see the fictional frats represented. But that's not the part that was most unexpected.

After some back-and-forth Sony agreed, at my urging, although they didn't have to, to make a donation of 2.5 percent from the opening-weekend proceeds of *Stomp the Yard* to the then in-progress Martin Luther King, Jr. Memorial in Washington, D.C. Huge. And in part because of the public noise from the threatened boycott, our opening weekend did big numbers, which meant a substantial donation to the memorial. To this day I can visit the incredible MLK Memorial and look on with a great deal of pride and tell my kids, "Your dad helped build that."

Years later a new administration of Alpha Phi Alpha led by president Skip Mason brought my line brother Rob Hardy—who executive produced *Stomp the Yard*—and me onstage in New Orleans at the Alpha national convention. He publicly thanked us for our contribution to the arts and for being the epitome of what it means to be an Alpha man. He apologized for the way the past administration treated us and awarded us lifetime membership status.

Triumph.

I told that story publicly for the first time in 2023, when I was honored by the MLK Memorial Foundation's Leaders of Democracy Awards in Washington, D.C. Talk about full circle. And that's why, boys and girls, we treat those two impostors just the same. Because your journey is ongoing, your story is still being written. Even in the darkest moments, remember it ain't over. My *Stomp the Yard* story wasn't completed when my own frat brothers tried to torpedo my movie and maybe my career, any more than it was over when I had people telling me how great the film was after early screenings.

There is no such thing as a total failure. There are moments when it may feel like it. But the reality is that there is always something positive that can be gleaned from a negative situation. Sometimes you just have to shift your perspective. Metaphorically tilt your head forty-five degrees and change your view. Then have the courage to look beyond the negative events that are happening in the short term.

And by the way, next time you're in D.C. swing by the MLK Memorial. On many levels and for many reasons that monument serves as an example of how something good can be gleaned from a negative situation. Tell 'em Dr. King's proud Alpha brother Will Packer sent you.

EVERY DISASTER ISN'T A FAILURE

The number of people who have executive produced an Academy Awards telecast is slim. It's an ultra-exclusive club, although it's debatable whether anybody really wants to be a member of it. It puts all the eyes of Hollywood on you, all the expectations of Hollywood on you, and all the toxicity of Hollywood on you. It's a thankless, backbreaking job. At the same time, it's super high-profile—the Mount Everest of live television producing. If there is one award show that people around the world pay at least a little bit of attention to, it's the Oscars. In that sense, being in charge of it is a crowning achievement, a major feather in your cap.

In another sense, award shows have long been a dying medium. Having your name on the biggest is like telling the world "I'm the one that can save the dinosaurs! No Steven Spielberg or special effects needed!" It means voluntarily heaping a ton of opinions, negativity, and unrealistic expectations upon your shoulders. In that sense, it's a no-win situation.

Soon after I accepted the job to produce the 94th Academy Awards, an officer within the academy, who had produced the infamous Oscar show when *La La Land* was mistakenly announced as Best Picture instead of *Moonlight*, tried to assuage me. "You'll be fine!" she insisted. "No matter what happens, it won't be as crazy as the year I did it."

I also spoke to my mentor Reggie Hudlin, who co-produced the Oscars previously. "You should do it," he said. "When you produce the Oscars, you're one of a very, very small group of people. It's a thing they put on your tombstone." I didn't realize that it might be the thing that would lead me to having a tombstone.

By now you're probably aware that I produced one of the most talked-about live shows in television history. Not because of the record-breaking amount of diversity in front of and behind the cameras. Not because of the historic Oscar wins for members of the deaf, LGBTQ, and Latin communities. But because an actor made a joke about another actor's wife and that actor slapped the first actor on live television. Freaking actors.

Ironically, the joke-cracking actor was one of my biggest proponents and gave me advice leading up to the show. "Will, don't try to do too much," he warned. "This show is hard. Just get the show done. Just land the plane, bro." *[Narrator: Even more irony that in that analogy he would play a role as one of the plane hijackers.]*

I had three main goals for the telecast: I wanted the ratings to finally go up after several years of steady decline. I wanted the show to come in under three hours. And I wanted Beyoncé again (she was nominated for Original Song for "Be Alive" from *King Richard*).

I was flat-out told, "Will, Beyoncé is not doing the Oscars. She loves you, but there's no version of her doing it." A resounding Fortuitous No. I had convinced her to do *Obsessed* after she said no years before, and I was hoping and praying I didn't burn my one Beyoncé yes.

Just like with *Obsessed*, I stopped at nothing to get Beyoncé to perform. She turned it down multiple times before finally agreeing to an idea that was pretty damn genius, if I say so myself. A pre-recorded performance at the Compton tennis courts, portrayed in the movie *King Richard,* where the tennis phenom Williams sisters had played as kids.

Although the show ran way over time as usual, in the end I accomplished two of my three goals—Beyoncé opened the show, and the ratings went up for the first time in years. All things considered, two out of three ain't bad. [*Narrator: For the record, the slap happened too late in the show to have a substantial effect on the ratings. Knowing Will (Packer), if he had seen it coming he would have moved it earlier.*]

At first, one of my biggest productions left me feeling very disappointed. With a little time and space, I was able to change my perspective and find pride and even levity in it. Shayla Cowan and I were the first all-Black producing team in Oscars history. Nothing can ever take that away. We produced a show that was bold and flavorful and took chances. Did it go exactly according to plan? Not at all. Am I super proud of that show? You better believe it. And do I have the absolute best story to tell at dinner parties? Without a doubt.

10

If It's on the Floor, It's the Floor's Money

What's for You Is for You. What's Not, Well . . . Isn't.

If you saw a hundred-dollar bill on the ground, you would pick it up, right? Sure, no-brainer. Grab it. Look around to see if it looks like anybody has a claim to it. If not, and a rightful owner can't realistically be found, then you're the rightful owner. Put it in your pocket and keep it moving while letting out a little "Won't *He* do it!"

But now imagine that you can only pick it up with your right hand and in that right hand you are clutching tight to a single dollar bill. By definition you have to let go of the dollar to grab the hundred. Still a no-brainer. But do you know how many people are metaphorically passing over hundreds while holding tightly to singles?

Letting go of things that aren't for us can be very difficult, even painful. Be it things in our past, people in our present, harmful ways of thinking, or habits that we know aren't good for us, letting go is tough. Especially if it's something that is comfortable and familiar. But it is essential for personal growth and vital for mental health. You have to remember . . . some things just aren't for you.

Now, let's talk about the hundreds that you *can't* pick up.

When I moved to Atlanta, I went to my first strip club. The experience was eye-opening and exhilarating, but not in the way you might think. I was enamored not so much with the *very* *ahem* talented entertainers but with the obsession with conspicuous consumption that was in evidence everywhere you looked. This was the famed Atlanta establishment Magic City. The name is quite apropos. They have "magicians" who are extremely adept at making things "disappear." Namely, your money. For years Monday night has been *the* happening night at Magic. Going to Magic City on a Monday night in the late nineties was like walking into a literal hurricane of dollars. This was the playground of professional athletes, rappers, corporate execs, celebs . . . anybody with access to money. And I don't mean exemplary lines of credit or impressive asset portfolios. I mean cold hard *cash*. And lots of it. That was the *only* thing that mattered on a Magic City Monday. Spending a bunch of money and making sure everybody *saw* you spend a bunch of money.

It's not lost on me that these (mostly) male ballers were paying most of their attention not to the scantily (and by *scantily* I'm referring to their shoes) clad women who were all around them but to the other men in the club to see who was spending the most. It was a full-on male-versus-male peacock fest, so to speak. And as a young, broke entrepreneur who barely had enough gas to put in my car for my paper route the next morning, this scene was mind-blowing.

Now, there is an understood rule in places such as this that no matter how much money is thrown, tossed, or otherwise projected, once it lands on the floor you *cannot* pick it back up . . . *ever*! Even if it's your own money and a wad slips out of your hand . . . Oh well, sorry, it's gone. I'm not sure how I knew this at the time but I did, and after somehow scraping up the money to pay the cover charge to get in I was left to be a spectator while the dudes with actual money showed out. I remember standing in the club one particular night, amazed at the circus I was witnessing. The club was packed to the gills. Literally, there were bodies (many clothed) wherever you turned. Guys were tossing trash bags full of money into the air so it would rain down everywhere with wild abandon. As I stood there with fifty- and hundred-dollar bills on the ground all around me, I had a single thought: "I could pay my rent for two months with what's at my feet right now." Grabbing one handful could have changed my life.

Out of temptation I stepped on a hundred-dollar bill and just left my foot there. I'm not sure what my plan was, but I suddenly wished I'd had the foresight to put double-sided tape on the bottom of my Nikes. As I stood there trying to figure out how to get the bill from the bottom of my shoe to my pocket, I noticed a grizzled, hulking bouncer staring right at me. He had seen my little move. He just looked at me and shook his head while not breaking eye contact, as if to say, "Don't even think about it, youngblood." It made me so nervous I slowly took my foot off the money and left immediately. I wasn't really having fun anyway. The place just reminded me how poor I was. I realized it was my time to level up. True, it looked like there was enough money on the floor of the club that night to *buy* one of the teams that half those dudes played for, but as Jeezy says, "If it's on the floor . . . it's the floor's money."

Don't covet things that aren't yours—whether you're swimming in Benjamins in a strip club or swimming in your fifteenth ill-fitting bridesmaid's dress wondering enviously, "When will it be my turn?" You're thinking, "I wish I could have that. I want that." But that's not for you. We've all had a moment of envy, gazing longingly at someone else's career, relationship, house, car. Those moments represent valuable time that could have been spent working toward attaining your own goals. Time you can never get back. What's for you is for you, and you have to make your own life, not someone else's. That also goes for anything that's not making you better, progressing you toward your own goals, or aligned with your future. Let that ish go.

That money was not mine. It was never going to be mine. It was not for me. Those people chose to irresponsibly throw a house note on the floor. They didn't choose to give me the money. They chose to toss it at the feet, heads, and other areas of attractive entertainers. That was their choice. Trying to change that or envying it would do me no good. I just needed to keep working hard so I could afford to irresponsibly waste money someday.

Never look at what somebody else has or what you don't have and say, "I should have that. I need that." Focus more on what you do have and how you can make that better. That's time and energy better spent because at least it's spent working *toward* something. And often that requires being willing to change the way you're doing things. You'll never reach lofty goals doing the same thing you've been doing; otherwise you would have reached them already. You have to be amenable to doing something different. Oftentimes that means something out of your comfort zone. Being uncomfortable is tough but well worth the reward of success, so go for it.

As far as we can prove, this is the only life we have, so you can't be afraid of uncharted waters—unless you believe in reincarnation, but even that is a crapshoot. What if you come back as an inanimate object, like, say, a hundred-dollar bill? And you end up stuck on the dirty floor of a strip club, begging to be picked up?! Too late now . . . you're the floor's money.

SOMETIMES IT'S OKAY TO QUIT

It's popular for people to say, "Never give up! Never say die!" Well, I'm here to tell you that there are some exceptions to that, times when it's more than okay to throw in the towel. Let's stick with the strip club theme, shall we? [Narrator: Do we have to?] In our struggling post-collegiate Atlanta days, when I was selling newspapers door-to-door and Rob was hawking Cutco knives and $2,500 vacuum cleaners to make ends meet, I had this genius idea of an easier way to make big money—cleaning strip clubs at the end of the night.

Sadly, this is not a joke. See, even though Rob and I were broke, sometimes we'd spend what little we had at the strip club. We didn't have much going for ourselves. The film thing was slow going. We needed a release. Whatever, it was a long time ago. Don't judge us! While there late one night, I looked around and blurted out, "We're going to start a janitorial company, but we're gonna clean strip clubs!" In my young mind that was a cool, sexy job. You get in the club for free. You're there when they close and get to hang out with the dancers after hours.

We called ourselves P&H Cleaning, for Packer and Hardy. P&H was an entrepreneurial, ambitious enterprise that lasted all of fifteen days. The strip club is a pleasure palace, a fantasy island; the vibes are flowing, the music is going . . . until the lights come on. Then it becomes one of the most disgusting places you can imagine. They flip that light switch and you're immediately Beyond the Wall in *Game of Thrones*.

The dancers did not hang out with us. They were like, "Boy, you are sweeping the floor. I'm not about to talk to you." As soon as the night ended, they took off their dance outfits and got back to being regular human beings who looked exhausted and just wanted to go home. I haven't even gotten to the worst part yet. So here we are at four A.M. with post-club-looking strippers booking past us out the door, and we'd have to clean up their dressing room. I can never unsee the things I saw in there. Tampons, dirty panties, and a smell I can only describe as an unfortunate combination of feet and ass.

Don't even get me started on the private rooms. It swore me

off of strippers for years. Okay, maybe more like months. Okay, actually weeks, but the point is I needed a break.

So yeah, two weeks after its founding, P&H Cleaning said, "We out." Sometimes an idea is worth abandoning. Sometimes you gotta give it up. Cut your losses. People are like, "Don't ever be a quitter." Those people haven't seen what I have. And a word of advice: Stay out of those private rooms.

11

Go Shawty, It's Ya Birthday

**Ownn Yoouurr Momenntt. Own Your Look.
Own Yourself.**

Perspective has a tangible effect on our ability to execute any task. The mentality you bring to the table shapes the outcome. This is a superpower we have within us that often goes untapped.

I vividly remember the day I was pitching an ensemble comedy film to Universal Pictures. I woke up with a fire in my belly that day. I woke up feeling invincible. I woke up feeling that I would not be denied. It didn't matter that I was about to appear in front of a tough room of Hollywood studio suits or that I would probably face all kinds of challenges trying to get my movie sold. It didn't matter that they'd heard a million other pitches that week. It didn't even matter that my time slot was right after lunch, when everybody's eyes are at half-mast because they need a nap. *{Narrator: Google "the itis." But for my white friends, don't actually use it. You're welcome.}* I remember that day so clearly because the date was April 11. Now, that date probably holds no significance for you, just like it held none for anybody else in that room. For them, it was just another Friday. But for me, it was a magical day—the day that William Edward Packer, Jr., first graced the earth with his presence. It was my birthday. On that day, I was unstoppable.

Now, sure, I was a little bummed I was working on my birthday and not on some tropical beach enjoying sun and libations. But it wouldn't be the first or last time April 11 fell on a day when I had important work stuff to do and I was in an exceptional mood, simply because of the date. I was excited about the fact that it was *my* special day. I felt strong. I felt confident. I felt like I could do no wrong and nothing could go wrong.

I'd gotten a haircut the day before, because haircuts make you confident. I put on an outfit that I just knew I looked good in. It can't be your birthday if you don't have a haircut and the right fit, right? Fresh blazer, dark jeans, leather belt matching my brown boots, and a newsboy cap tilted just right. I looked at myself in the mirror more than twice and said, "I'm going to win today."

I always tell my kids, "Own your moment. Own your look. Own yourself." Own every stage you stand on and every room you walk into. If you're on a video conference, own that little square others see you in. If you feel good about it, it's pervasive. It's contagious. Other people will feel your energy and passion and emulate it.

I took my fresh fade, fresh fit, and fresh energy right into the pitch meeting. When I walked into that room, I brought all my passion and determination with me. I went in with this mentality of "I don't care whether they want to hear this or not, they're going to love it. They're going to buy it. Because I will be damned if I have to work on my birthday and not come out of this meeting successful. Today of all days, I'm going to kill it. I'm walking in the birthday boy and walking out a champion. April 11 is a day when Will Packer succeeds. Period."

I pitched my ass off. I presented a story about four sexy, strong, yet flawed Black female friends who attend a music festival in New Orleans. The story was loosely based on how I met my wife at the real-life Essence Fest. I laid it out succinctly and thoroughly on a silver platter. I gave it everything I had, leaving no doubts about my vision. I was humorous, enthralling, and confident from moment one, and they ate it up with a spoon. It was one of my best "performances" ever in a room. When I'm in the zone like that, I call it going "full Packer." That's my personal video game superhero mode. I was charismatic, thoughtful, and undeniable. And it was all driven by my state of mind. I came in guns blazing and it worked. Needless to say, they bought it. And that pitch, *Girls Trip,* ultimately turned into one of my biggest movies ever.

Weeks later, I remember feeling a little anxious about another big meeting I had coming up. I thought, "It's too bad I don't have that birthday mojo—too bad I can't go 'full Packer' for this meeting." As if I had unlocked some secret birthday genie who had sprinkled success dust on me the morning of April 11 while sounding a lot like a cross between Robin Williams and Will Smith. *{Narrator: Bold choice to mix Aladdin references there.}*

The reality is it wasn't about a date on the calendar at all. My mojo had nothing to do with April 11. That pitch could have been February 19. It could have been November 3. That's not the point. The point is that I came in with a mentality of "I am going to win today because today is *my* day. I can't lose no matter what. I may lose tomorrow, but today . . . I win."

Now I ask you, what is stopping us from doing that consistently? From unlocking that perspective? From having the mentality that we deserve this energy not only today but on any particular day? The truth is, we all have the power within us to unleash that confidence whenever we want. Today *could* be your birthday. What if we treat every important day like it's our birthday? What's stopping you from going "full Packer"? *{Narrator: Well, let's say "full <insert your name here>." You going "full Packer" would just be weird.}*

When you're gearing up for a major performance, presentation, or challenge, you should mentally force yourself into your best zone, and by the time you finish you should be exhausted because you put everything into it. You should walk in feeling like you cannot lose and walk out feeling like you've won. No matter what.

I always feel like I should be drained at the end of my pitch meetings because I should be so passionate about it. I challenge myself to be deadly earnest about the exact reason why the financier unequivocally must buy this. I go in feeling like they *have* to back this movie because this is the *one,* it's going to make *money,* it's going to win *awards,* whatever their main goal is. Usually money. And I must really believe it to the point where they believe it too. Because if I don't believe it, why should they? And in Hollywood, often a movie has to be pitched multiple times after I pitch it. The creative execs may love it, but they have to sell it to marketing, they have to sell it to the international team, if the head of the studio isn't in the room somebody has to sell it to them. And it's like the game of telephone: Everything gets diluted the more hands it goes through. So, if I don't believe it that steadfastly and that passionately, how am I going to get someone else to then believe it with that same level of energy and passion so they can sell it to whoever they have to sell it to?

Your perspective can manifest success. You have the power; you just need to unlock it. It starts the minute you wake up. Wake up thinking about how you are going to win today. Let that be the overriding thought that carries you through the day. I have my own daily affirmation. I stand in front of the mirror every morning and tell myself how primed I am, how capable I am, how well prepared I am for the day and the tasks at hand. I tell myself how I am fully equipped with the skill set necessary to accomplish everything I need to accomplish that day.

There are two reasons I do this: Number one, it will probably be the last time I hear it that day. I mean, who else is going to tell me that? I need to hear that. I make sure that I hear it at least once. Number two, I say it so that I can believe it. I say it to myself because I know I'm going to hear a lot of voices throughout the day, but I also know that I'm the most important voice I will hear that day. Not somebody I'm pitching to, or a boss, or a spouse, or a child. No, it's me, my voice. They may all have value in my life, but none more valuable than me. So, I'm hearing positivity from the most important person in my life, and I'm starting the day with it.

That positive affirmation to start the day gives me momentum. I used to tell my kids at the start of the school year, "Come in strong! Start hot! Don't come in like, 'Aight, I'll get there. I got time.'" I remind them if they're running a race, it's easier if you're ahead in first place and everybody's trying to catch you and harder to catch up when you're behind, looking at the soles of somebody's shoes. Start the day ahead of the game. Start ahead of the competition. They may not have heard how great they are from the most important person in their life, but you did.

Have you ever heard the saying "Help the bear"? If you see me in a fight with a bear, help the bear. Pour honey on me. That's a winner's mentality, the mentality you need to have to not just beat whatever your "bear" may be but to *destroy* that damn bear. You have to believe you are the best. That you've got what it takes. I tell myself that every day, and it doesn't matter if I don't hear it again. I believe it, even if nobody else does.

I went into the *Girls Trip* pitch like I had some secret power that day, because it happened to be April 11. But I know that I can unlock that, if I put my mind to it, any of the other 364 days of the year. Don't allow external factors to define your day. Don't wake up and think, "Oh, today's going to be a rough day." Stop right there. Does it have to be a bad day? Don't even allow that thinking. Even with everything you're up against and all the challenges that await, this could be the most amazing day ever. What if you go in and exceed any expectations you or anyone else had for you that day? Redefine what this day and this date means for you. You have that power. Do not allow superficial and external things to define your perspective. Some people hate April 15 because it's tax day. But to an

accountant it's payday. Shift your point of view. We all find ourselves slipping into a negative mindset from time to time. Pay attention to that so you can self-correct right away. Be wary of allowing
one negative thought to turn into ten. Change your mentality to
something affirming at the first sign of defeatism.

A positive mindset extends beyond a single day on the calendar. In my personal life I've come to embrace the idea of celebrating
my actual birthday at different times throughout the year depend-
ing on what's going on in my life. Sometimes life's circumstances
align in a way that makes it more practical to celebrate later or earlier than on my actual birthday. And you know what? That's perfectly fine. Sometimes shooting schedules or life events dictate when
I can gather friends and loved ones to mark the occasion.

But birthdays, like life itself, don't have to be confined to a
single day. We have the power to celebrate whenever it feels right,
whenever it aligns with our circumstances and brings us the most
fulfillment. It's about the mentality we bring, the intention we set,
and the elements we assemble to make the moment truly special. It
all starts in our minds, and in the way we think about and perceive
the world. We have the ability to manufacture favorable circumstances, to create moments of joy and fulfillment. Try embracing the
mentality of possibility, and watch as your experiences transform
into something truly extraordinary.

Stand in front of the mirror no matter what the calendar says
and tell yourself that today is *your* day, the day you're going to conquer the world!

12

So What If You Miss the Flight?

Achieving Is Good, but Joy Is Better

You wanna be *great?* Find your joy. I've been a pretty solid achiever for most of my life. But only recently have I been able to truly unlock my own joy. To achieve, you have to be driven, you have to be relentless, you have to be willing to work yourself to almost (figurative) death. But real happiness requires an understanding that doing all the aforementioned only matters in the right balanced mix of priorities. My family helps me keep those priorities straight on a daily basis.

There is no question that my wife Heather makes me a happier person. I am also one thousand percent certain that my wife has made me a better man and husband. She was a missing piece in my life. One of Heather's best qualities is that as much as we have in common, in many ways she's the exact opposite of me. Heather Packer is often very measured and chill; Will Packer often . . . is not. Will Packer is constantly plugged in. He may or may not have brought his cellphone into the shower before. Heather Packer could not look at her phone for days, which is both impressive and maddening, if you're Will Packer. Heather is perpetually late because she's not very time-conscious. While that's not necessarily a good thing, it's actually not a bad balance for me because I can be time-obsessive. Constantly dealing with productions where millions are on the line and time is literally money has made me like that. If I'm being honest, sometimes I don't turn it off.

One time my wife and I were cutting it too close to catch a flight. I could feel the stress building up within me. I had planned ahead, told her we needed to leave at an earlier time than we actually did, all my usual strategies I use because . . . I know my wife. We were still about to miss this damn flight. I watched as she not-hurriedly-enough finished her meal. Beads of sweat forming on my forehead. Why is she eating? We don't have time to eat. And she's chewing too? Okay, you either gotta chew the food or swallow it; there's no time for both. We're going to miss our plane!

It was at that moment that a voice inside me asked a simple question: "What if you miss this flight?" My anxious analytical mind kicked into overdrive, calculating the consequences of missing the flight, the rearrangements, the rescheduling, the inconveniences. Then I took a second and did a recalculation from a different, more relaxed, methodical point of view. Turns out, missing this particular flight wouldn't actually flip my world upside down the way that I thought. As I played out the scenarios in my mind, I realized it wouldn't be the life-altering failure I made it out to be. In fact, it wouldn't even be that bad and there was actually some benefit to a forced rearranging of the schedule that day. Then I balanced that against the stress I was putting on myself, on my wife, on our relationship—it wasn't even close to being worth it. I said, "You know what, honey, finish your meal. It's gonna be just fine."

She gave me a look in a way that only a Black woman can that said, "Yeah, I'm glad you figured that out. And you know I was going to finish my meal," as she took another bite.

Sometimes we get so caught up in the pressures of achievement and the ancillary challenges it brings that we get our priorities and perspectives out of whack. I was with my son Dom a few years ago when he and one of his friends were exchanging "worst pain you ever felt" stories. Dom's was about when he had surgery in high school due to a football injury. He was talking about the awful recovery and how his grandmother had to help him get to the bathroom.

"Excuse me," I interrupted. "First of all, the pain should be the embarrassment of having Grammy take you to pee. You're supposed to be an athlete!" His friend snickered. "Secondly, I remember that surgery. Why was Grammy there with you? Where was I?"

"You had a trip to L.A."

"What? I literally remember when you got the surgery."

"Yeah, you were there when I had surgery. Then you had to fly out the next day. That whole awful week of recovery I was with Grammy."

He remembered it vividly and kept going on with other cringey details. "Damn," I thought. "The most physically painful moment of my son's life and I wasn't there." He wasn't accusing me of anything, mind you. Me not being there wasn't even important to the story. It was just a matter of fact for him. But I couldn't stop thinking about it. This was a time in my child's life that he will never, ever forget. And you could pay me a trillion dollars and I guarantee you I couldn't remember what it was that pulled me to L.A. that particular week and had me fly my mom in while my son recovered.

I chose to live, work, and raise my family in Atlanta and not L.A. I made that decision early on in my career. It seemed counterintuitive to many of my Hollywood peers. But for me, raising my kids in an environment that didn't feel like such a closed-off bubble of families, friends, and social networks all centered on the same industry was a no-brainer. Plus, I loved raising my Black kids in a city like Atlanta, where African Americans are seen at every level of the economic, governmental, and community power structure.

Because I made that choice, I was always flying back and forth across the country. This was nothing new. And whatever I had to do in L.A. the week of Dom's surgery, I'm sure it felt important at the time. But I'm also very, very sure that if I had missed whatever it was and stayed that week with my kid, nobody in Hollywood would've remembered what I missed. Nobody.

Dom will, for the rest of his life, remember the week that his dad wasn't there. He may not harbor resentment, but that was a major time for him. And I realized it, by chance, in that moment as he and his friend exchanged mildly impressive affliction stories. "Okay," I thought, "I have to really look at my priorities because stuff gets canceled, moved around, and reprioritized all the time in our business."

Now, I'm not saying you shouldn't be driven, accountable, and willing to fly across the country when you need to. You have to be focused, you have to deliver, you have to be on time, you have to make the meetings, all of that. But if I had canceled some meeting to spend time with my child during an important period, even if it was with the president of a movie studio, they'd probably have been like, "All right, we'll do it another week or you can call in, no biggie." But they definitely wouldn't have remembered that meeting years later. I certainly don't.

That was an awakening. I realized I should have prioritized that moment in my child's life. That was a mistake I can't take back. Sometimes you gotta ask, "So what if I miss the flight?"

Success often requires going a million miles an hour fearlessly around hairpin curves careening on two wheels. Happiness sometimes requires you to give yourself permission to slow down, take your time, breathe, and enjoy the journey. Some people are more intrinsically built toward the latter. Some in my own family.

When my youngest son, Zion, was ten, I took him to a go-kart birthday party for one of his friends. I was immediately jealous because we didn't have these types of go-karts when I was growing up. These kids at this party were in actual bona fide mini race cars. They had to be going twenty to twenty-five miles per hour. It didn't look particularly safe at all. But, boy, did it look fun. I was watching all the kids zooming around, racing one another and having a high-speed blast. All except Zion. My son was going at a snail's pace, like he was stuck in slow motion. Naturally, as a concerned dad, I went straight to the guy running the track, full of indignation. I was like, "Hey, are all the go-karts working properly? Look at my son; he's practically standing still while everyone else is passing him. I paid the same as everyone else. I can't have my son in the slowest go-kart!"

The guy, probably used to dealing with dads like me, kinda rolled his eyes and said, "They're all preset to run at the same speed, sir. We check them every morning."

"Umm, well, obviously, Mr. Go-Kart Technician, you missed one when you checked them. You see what I see. Look at Marvin," I said, pointing at one of Zion's friends whizzing around the track. "Marvin is on two wheels about to die every time he goes around a curve. I want my kid to be Marvin. I want my kid to almost die too!"

He stared at me silently, like "Are you serious?"

I stared at him silently back, like "Umm, yeah. Fix this mane."

{*Narrator: The word* mane *is Memphis slang for "man." Will's wife Heather is from Memphis. There are no coincidences. As you were.*}

He motioned for Zion to pull over to the side and had him get out of the car while he checked the engine and the gas pedal on the cart. They had a little chat, but they were out of earshot so I couldn't make out what he was saying. I just saw Zion smile and then they both turned and looked at me and laughed. Then Zion got back in the car and started driving again . . . *at the same speed.*

Go-Kart Gary *{Narrator: Definitely not his name}* came over to me and said, "Sir, the go-kart is perfectly fine. Your son is choosing to go slow."

I was dumbfounded. I also didn't know if I really believed this guy. The next time Zion got close to my side of the track, I leaned over and looked very closely as he drove past. He was going so slow that I could clearly see his foot was barely pressing the gas pedal.

"Zion!" I yelled. "Are you good? Are you having fun? Why aren't you going faster?"

With a mischievous grin, he gave me a big thumbs-up and replied, "Dad, I'm good. I'm having fun. I don't need to go fast."

"Ummm, okay, son," I said reluctantly as he slow-poked away.

While I was ready to give the go-kart people a piece of my mind, my son was content with his leisurely pace. He didn't care about winning or keeping up with the others. I realized that Zion was just built differently. He was comfortable going at his own pace, and there was something truly admirable about that.

Zion taught me an important lesson that day, that everybody enjoys life differently. Don't try to impose your method of enjoyment on other people. If I want to drive my go-kart full speed into a pile of tires and have back problems for the rest of my life, that's fine for me. But Zion, like a lot of people, doesn't want that. He showed me in his characteristic, unbothered-by-the-need-for-speed way that not everything has to be a race.

Zion, Dom—my girls too—have taught me to slow down and refocus my priorities. I'm watching and listening to them. Just a side note on the flip side: You think your kids aren't listening to you, but they are. I promise you. I didn't think my kids listened to one thing I have said ever in my life, never took anything I said seriously. I felt like I was wasting all these gems. However, as they're getting older they will recite things back to me that I've said to them. They're doing things in their lives and they'll say, "Yeah, because, you know, you always say . . ." You guys always act like you're not paying attention. You're paying attention?! *Insert single Denzel Washington in *Glory* tear.*

My wife also helps me with balance. Somebody that helps give you balance, whether it's a life partner or a friend or a business partner, that's important. The best people that I've worked with were people who saw the world differently from me, and it made me better. Because of course I think everybody should see the world the way I see it. But thank God they don't. When I work with people who see it differently, it helps open my mind.

Because of all of them, I've found a way to work smarter rather than harder. And it's changed my approach as a leader, as a producer, and, most importantly, as a family man.

You know how when you get proven right and you can't wait for that person who was loud and wrong to acknowledge that you were right all along? After Zion gave me the thumbs-up and drove away, out of the corner of my eye I could see Go-Kart Gary staring at me, waiting on me to look at him so I would see the smug look on his face. He stared at me for like ten whole minutes, and I just stood there stubbornly refusing to acknowledge him. Finally, I just walked off. "I don't have time for this," I said. "I got a flight to catch."

THE FLIGHT I WISH I'D MISSED

I fly *a lot*. I'm a *Triple* Million Miler just on Delta Airlines alone. I'm currently writing this sidebar from a plane. *[Narrator: True story.]* One of the ways I earned all those miles was in an attempt to be a great father. My parents always made all my games and events when I was growing up, so despite the fact that I was often across the country working in Los Angeles, I vowed to do the same with my kids. No matter what I was working on, I would fly back to Atlanta every Friday during high school football season to make my son Dom's games. He excelled on the field and went on to play college football at Harvard. Clearly, that's largely because of the support of his dear old dad. *[Narrator: It was largely because of Dom's own drive and perseverance. But Will definitely supported.]*

It didn't go quite the same way with my youngest, Maya, when she was little. It was important to support all my kids equally, so I would fly into town for her five-year-old soccer games, hoping she would appreciate the lengths her dad went to and perform accordingly. *[Narrator: She was five.]* I vividly remember standing on the soccer field sidelines right after getting off a cross-country red-eye flight and watching in angst as my sweet angel would stand completely uninterested as other kids ran right by her up and down the field at least attempting to play soccer. I pulled her to the side.

"Do you know where Daddy just came from?"

"Los Angeles," she replied in her sweet preschool voice.

"And do you know where that is?"

"A long way away!"

"That's right. So since Daddy came from such a long way, would you just *try* to kick the ball, baby?"

"Yes, sir!"

Cut to Maya back on the field even less interested than before. In fact, after our "talk," the ball actually rolled up and hit Maya on the foot. Do you know, my child stared at that ball like "What is this? And why is it touching me? Somebody come get this thing."

Ugggh. Sometimes I wondered whether my children even loved me. *[Narrator: Again, she was five.]*

I digress. The point is I fly all the time so I've seen all kinds of things happen on flights. Passenger fights, crazy turbulence, emergency landings, you name it. One time I was on a flight when somebody in the back of the plane died of an apparent heart attack. I never saw anything, because it was a big plane and they took the person off from the back. So that time I was kind of shielded from it, but I was certainly aware tragedy had struck on the flight. However, this time, God was like, "I'm gonna let you see some harsh midair reality, Will Packer."

I was on a flight to Exuma, Bahamas, with Heather, probably thirty minutes from landing, when the woman in front of me started shaking violently . . . then just stopped. It happened so fast that I was just like, "Wait, did that happen? Did I imagine that? Wait. Oh my God. Ma'am. Ma'am?" Unresponsive. This was a very small plane because Exuma is a small Caribbean island.

This woman's name was Carol. I'll never forget her name because her husband kept saying it. These are older people. Let's say this woman is eighty-five-plus years old. The husband is at least her age or older. It becomes apparent that they're traveling by themselves and know no one else on the flight. The flight crew realizes she's had a seizure and is unresponsive.

There happened to be four doctors on board. Which is kinda insane because it was a plane of like forty people. The doctor-to-passenger ratio was crazy. But that's the type of people who travel to exotic locales, I guess. I was one of the people trying to help lift Carol and take her to the narrow aisle. I felt so powerless because she was so heavy. And this was an average-size woman, not particularly big. But she was total deadweight. We were trying to get her up from the seat to the aisle and it was just so awkward. She's this old lady, with a dress on, and you've got me and three other guys trying to lift her, and her arms are flailing and her dress flies up. Poor Carol did not intend to be seen that way on that day. That's the thing you don't see in the movies, the full awkwardness of these moments.

We finally lay her down and the doctors start giving oxygen and doing chest compressions. She's not responding at all. You could feel the dread start to creep in as the doctors look at one another helplessly with grim expressions. The rest of us were doing the best we could to get the husband to tell us anything. *Does she have a medical condition? Is she on medication? How old is she?* The husband wasn't answering. He was in total shock. He just kept calling his wife's name over and over and over again. He's like, "Carol, Carol, Carrrooolllll." It was clear he didn't really understand what was happening. He was calling to her like she was watching TV in the family room and he was trying to get her attention. I was thinking, "Oh my God, sir, she's dead. Carol's gone and you just keep saying her name."

I was praying, holding Heather's hand. Heather was holding a random woman's hand across the aisle who turned out to be the heir of the Wendy's Company. It wasn't Wendy, but it was Wendy's sister. Next best thing. Again, that's the type of people who travel to exotic locales. Doctors and fast food heiresses. If she had any clogged arteries from testing Pretzel Baconators, she was covered.

I was like, "Please, God, save this woman somehow." Because Exuma is small, the pilot had to divert to the next major city, Nassau, once they realized she might not make it. They wanted to get her to the closest major hospital. But by now we were already in our descent to Exuma. Like I said, I fly a lot. But I have never been so scared on a plane in my life because as we're descending, the pilot has to basically put on air brakes, lift the nose, and turn 180 degrees all at the same time. The mix of turbulence, cabin pressure, and centrifugal force was insane. I went so fast from "Please, Jesus, please don't take Carol!" to "Please, God, don't take *us*! If you gotta take somebody, God, Carol's old. She's lived a life. Don't sacrifice the rest of us. Please!"

The plane shook. It dropped. It turned. It shook some more. It was the worst. Oh my God, we're all gonna die. You could hear audible gasps and shrieks from the passengers. The husband is still in shock, saying, "Carrrroolllll . . ." I'm thinking, "Mister, *Carol's gonna kill all of us.*" I went from feeling so sorry for this woman and her husband to thinking, "Should we push them out of the emergency exit?! Pilot, you can't take us all down!"

So we survived this crazy hairpin turn, got on the ground in Nassau, and the ambulance came screeching up. The paramedics came on board and, guess what? Carol starts breathing again. She's alive. Carol's alive to this day, as far as I know.

We ended up in Nassau for over six hours because when something like this happens you gotta do all this paperwork, you gotta refill the oxygen, et cetera. Carol was alive but still very much out of it and not super responsive. But they did get her to say her name. "Carol, Carol, Carol . . ."

If that near-death experience taught me anything, it is that it doesn't matter if you're a Three, Four, or Five Million Miler with your airline. Ultimately, that's not nearly as gratifying as being alive to watch your five-year-old treat a soccer ball like she owes it money.

13

The Only Bad Thing About Being First Is Being First

Regret Is Worse Than Failure

Have you ever had the opportunity to be the first to do something? For some people it can be the thrill of a lifetime to hear, "No one has ever successfully climbed that mountain" or "No one has ever swum across that alligator-infested river." They think, "Wow, I can be the first!" However, most sane folks realize, "Wellllll, there is probably a really good reason no one has ever done said perilous task before." The same is true of being the first of a particular category: first African American, first woman, first LGBTQ'r, first disabled person . . .

It *sounds* cool to be the first anything, until you're that person and you realize, "I got no peers. There hasn't been anybody like me I can look to and say that they've done this and survived. Am I crazy? Can I do it? Is it meant to be?" It takes extreme mental fortitude and courage to be "the first."

I know how hard it can be to be the first, but ultimately I look at the possible payoff being worth it every time—except maybe swimming across those alligator-infested waters. What I've come to learn about my dad really helped bring this lesson home. There were a lot of reasons I looked up to him, but one of the big ones was because of Winn-Dixie. My father grew up very poor in Panama City, Florida. When he needed to help support his mother and grandmother financially, he applied for a job at the local grocery store, Winn-Dixie. Problem was, this Winn-Dixie didn't have any Black employees. Never had. This was not shocking. I mean, *Dixie* is right there in the name. *{Narrator: Cracker Barrel gets a pass in the pantheon of racially coded branding, because those pancakes are sublime.}*

People in my dad's neighborhood told him, "Don't even bother," because everyone knew Winn-Dixie was as white as a casting call for a special ski trip episode of *Friends*. But my father was determined. He needed the money, and he, being the Packer male that he was, believed he could overcome any obstacle thrown his way. So, one day, when he was about twelve, my dad waltzed right into the Winn-Dixie and told the manager that he wanted to be a bag boy. The manager smirked, and with a patronizing twinkle in his eye told Pops, "Sure, all you have to do is pass an advanced math test to get a job here." This Winn-Dixie apparently had its own iteration of the post–Civil War "literacy tests." Instead of not wanting Black folks to register to vote in the South, they didn't want them to pack potatoes and milk into a sack.

"No problem," said my dad. "When can I take the test?"

The manager played along. He showed my dad a sample test, which of course was a complicated, high school senior–level mathematics exam. It was totally absurd; the young white baggers working there surely didn't know what a binomial equation was—heck, do you think they even knew the difference between butter lettuce and Bibb lettuce? *{Narrator: That's a trick question. There is no difference between butter lettuce and Bibb lettuce.}* It was doubtful the manager could even pass his own math test. But seeing that my dad was undeterred, the guy actually set a date for the following week. Whether the manager was impressed with my dad's cantaloupe-sized cojones or just bored, we'll never know. What we do know is that he expected this young Black boy to slink out of the store with his tail between his legs and never come back. Let's just say, that's not what happened.

My dad studied day and night, poring over math problems that were far beyond his years, getting help where he could from teachers perplexed as to why he was doing all this work. And guess what? He passed that dang test—and the manager kept his word and through gritted teeth hired his first Black employee at the Winn-Dixie. Black folks from surrounding counties would drive to that store just to see the first Black bagger. "Here you go, baby," they'd say, and tip him five cents. He became a local legend.

Now, my dad never told me that story before he passed away. He also never talked to me about being the first Black engineering graduate of the University of South Florida. It's not that he was Mr. Quiet Humble Guy. He was confident and proud. Such a Packer. But those just weren't the things he bragged about. My mom did it for him. But even with my mom, it was never, "Sit down, I'm gonna blow your mind with this story!" It was really matter-of-fact divulgences told between cooking spaghetti in the kitchen and getting my sister and me ready for Sunday school.

To truly appreciate my dad's rebel spirit you have to understand from whence he came. I didn't learn until very recently that my granddaddy Packer also was a bit of a maverick. As a kid growing up, I would catch pieces of adult conversations about Granddaddy. *On the run, Alabama,* and *Klan* were words I distinctly remember. But I knew better than to ask questions. A few years ago, I was at a family reunion when my uncle Thomas finally told me the inspiring and tragic backstory. Granddaddy grew up in Alabama, and when he was about twenty, he was working on the railroad when a truckload of racist drunk white boys drove up to him holding rifles. "Dance, [n-word]," they demanded.

Granddaddy Packer was tough and hard, so he told them in so many words to kick rocks. *{Narrator: Will may not curse much in* *this book, but you* know *Granddaddy Packer did.}* Well, the white boys didn't like that. They aimed their guns at Granddaddy's feet and sprayed bullets, so he didn't have a choice but to dance. After they had their fun, they told him to get out of there and proceeded to continue drinking. But Granddaddy Packer wasn't the kind to forgive and forget. He went and grabbed a crowbar, went right back down to the same spot, snuck up on them, and beat the living daylights out of all four of those white boys at the same time. He beat three within an inch of their lives. One didn't survive.

Word traveled like wildfire that Packer killed a white boy. Ku Klux Klan members from four towns away began throwing on bedsheets. His brothers went to his house and searched the town frantically looking for him, but he was nowhere to be found. They finally stumbled upon him chilling at a bar, unfazed, enjoying a cold one.

"You gotta get outta here!" they pleaded. "The Klan is looking for you!"

"I ain't goin' nowhere."

"They will kill your mom and burn this whole town down. Let's go."

The brothers forcefully grabbed Granddaddy and literally carried him down to the train tracks. All the while he's kicking and screaming, "Put me down! I ain't leaving!" When a train rolled by, they threw him into the first open boxcar. They tossed him so hard, they thought he flew out the other side. But after the train passed, Granddaddy Packer was gone, and they never saw him again. Sure enough, the Klan came to his house and warned, "If he ever steps foot in Alabama again, we're stringing him up on the highest tree."

The train's last stop happened to be Panama City, Florida, and Granddaddy Packer was able to blend into the crowd. You used to be able to do that, disappear and start a new life, when there were no cellphones, security cameras, or John Walshes hunting down criminals on *America's Most Wanted.* He met my grandmother, they had kids, including my dad, and lived a happy, productive life there until he passed, the whole time carrying this extraordinary yet heavy secret.

That tale pretty much sums up the Packer mentality. Packer men are proud men. Packer men are fearless. When I heard that story it made total sense. I believed every word because I know my dad and I know me. Packer men all have that fire in our bellies. My dad was definitely that guy's son. And I'm definitely my dad's son.

Both my granddaddy and my pops were renegades. They stood up for themselves and did the things others were scared to do. We happened to be one of the first Black families to move into the neighborhood where I grew up in St. Petersburg, Florida. As soon as we moved in, someone left a threatening, racist letter and a rotting dead fish on our doorstep. I was only three years old at the time but, apparently, my father got his gun and sat outside all night on the porch, daring the bigot to come by again. My mom loves to tell the story that my dad fell asleep on the porch, gun sitting on his lap, so she went out there at four A.M. to wake him up and bring him inside. "They're just gonna shoot you with your own gun!" she teased. My mom still lives in that house to this day.

So, now that you know some of my family history, you can only care about that so much before you fairly ask, "What does this mean for me, in my own life?" Asking that doesn't make you self-centered; it makes you human. Here's my answer: Whether you're an entrepreneur or an electrical engineer, here's what I'd love for you to take away about attempting to do something daring:

You have to understand that the possibility of success should outweigh the fear of failure. And you have to be willing to ignore that fear and put everything into trying to make that success happen. Is there an opportunity for failure? A thousand percent. Absolutely. For instance, I could have been somebody who missed my window to use my college engineering degree and blew all my chances to be gainfully employed in that field, if Hollywood didn't work out for me.

But the *idea* of the possibility of success drove me. What if the movie thing worked out? What if I made a bunch of number-one movies? What if I broke records in Hollywood?! The *thought* of achieving wild triumph made navigating the perils worth the effort. Ask yourself, "Is the absolute most awful thing in the world that could happen if I fail possible?" Yes. "Will that worst-case scenario happen?" Probably not. "Is the upside of success totally worth it?" Abso-freaking-lutely.

Regret is worse than failure. The regret has always terrified me more than the thought of falling short. If you never even try? Man oh man, what a shame. That's death to me. I obsess over avoiding that awful feeling of regretting not trying. You should too.

Here's the other thing: Striving to do something great will make your life better, regardless of the outcome. You're a better person for having tried.

There's no question that being "the first" is a remarkable accomplishment, but it can also be a burdensome albatross. BIPOC and LGBTQ folks often become automatic and unwitting spokespeople for their tribes. On the other hand, if you're a straight white kid, I feel for you because somebody who looks like you has literally done everything that could possibly be done already. So if that's your demographic, you're out of luck. I'm kidding. Sort of.

Let me just point out that it's not *only* about being literally first. It's also about having a first-place mentality. You just have to be your best at something. Something daring. Something challenging. It's really about accomplishing a thing that isn't easy or traditional. Moses General Miles, who founded the chapter of my fraternity at my alma mater Florida A&M, has a famous quote: "If you can't be first, you sure better be ahead of whoever's second." The point is, be number one in *your* world. By the way, that fraternity, Alpha Phi Alpha, is the very *first* Black Greek letter organization, because of course it is.

I took Moses General Miles's quote very seriously. It was what drove me to make *Chocolate City*. While I did start at Florida A&M on an electrical engineering scholarship, just like my dad, deep down I always knew I really wanted to be an entrepreneur. At first I didn't know what kind, but then second semester of sophomore year, I was making plans with fellow engineering student Rob Hardy, who was already a budding filmmaker. It was his crazy idea to make a movie about a student's journey from boyhood to manhood at an HBCU. And I quickly zeroed in that this was a possible direction for me too.

Was he the first Black director or I the first Black producer of all time? No, there is a long history of Black filmmakers and trailblazers, like Oscar Micheaux, Spike Lee, the Hudlin brothers, and more. But were Rob and I the first to make a nationally distributed movie at an HBCU while students? Yes, we were. I'm very proud of that. I do always say I'm "the first" with the caveat that I could only do it because someone else opened a door for me. Giving credit to the torchbearers doesn't take away from the accomplishment of your own "first."

A lot of people looked at Rob and me like we were nuts. I just took solace in the fact that all pioneers are a little, ummm, off. The vibe with a lot of our classmates was, "If that's what you choose to do with your weekends—do you. The rest of us are going to go get drunk and watch the band play at the football game. Or we're going to the frat party, or we're going to go chase girls. But if you choose to be over here with a bunch of grungy dudes from Florida State film school up at six in the morning shooting until midnight with dusty old equipment, have at it!" It wasn't the popular thing to do. Nobody took it that seriously. Nobody thought a career would be born out of it.

Let the naysayers just fuel your fire. Just eat the negativity; you know, like an Internet troll. To make a movie, especially back then, you had to have money, lots of it. We didn't have any, just a dream and a bunch of electromechanics and circuit theory homework.

We needed donations. We lobbied the student government and the National Pan-Hellenic Council of all the Greek fraternities and sororities. I was in student government and Rob and I were Alphas, so we thought we had it made. These were our homies, right? No, sir. The hardest money to ever raise was from those students. You would have thought we were asking for the deed to the university. They made us come back several times and raked us over the coals. People who were my friends, who I'd been partying with the night before, were like, "Mr. Packer, please present your thesis and explain why we should support you."

"Dave . . . seriously? I literally carried you to your dorm after you did shots of Goldschläger last night."

"Rules of order! I have the floor. Answer the question, Mr. Packer!"

It was tough, but we were relentless; we got a few thousand dollars and we made the movie. That process prepared me for later in life when I had to go in front of intimidating suits at major Hollywood studios. They had nothing on hungover college students with a point to prove.

There was no established pathway for what we did, but we just kept cutting through the weeds with a machete. We had to make our own way. And whenever you are doing something for the first time, you are always going to run into challenges that seem insurmountable. But you have to have faith that the payoff is worth the efforts of finding a way past them.

The reward is usually universal; it benefits more than just you personally. The bottom line is that not only did my father's courage get him a job at Winn-Dixie, it also worked out for the grocery store. They got a trusty employee who was intelligent and hardworking. They also got new customers who came to see the Black bag boy.

Doing something untraditional is often going to be cold and lonely and uncomfortable, but that's not a bad thing. Embrace entering uncharted territory. There's a line from the documentary *Free Solo* I love that really drives this point home. The main guy, Alex Honnold, was the first person to scale El Capitan in Yosemite National Park without a rope, which is considered one of the greatest athletic achievements of all time. At one point, he says, "Anyone can be happy and cozy. Nothing good happens in the world by being happy and cozy." He's right on point—and by the way, I guess I was wrong about straight white guys not having anything left to do first. My bad.

No matter what you look like or what your upbringing was, going first is going to be scary. From the moon landing to Barack Obama, if someone doesn't have the guts to risk being first, we'd never make any progress on this planet. Somebody has to be the one to break the barrier and push the physical and ideological boundaries.

Who better than you? Go 'head with your great self.

I FAILED IT. I FAILED THIS CHAPTER.

So, here I am telling you to dare to be different. Stand out. Be courageous. I talk as if I was born thinking this way. I wasn't. Let me tell you about the time I just wanted to blend in with the crowd.

I played the trumpet for like thirty seconds in elementary school. I started because I really wanted to play in the school band. I always felt like the band kids were cool, especially the drummers. But my mom made it clear she wasn't having all that noise in her house. I had taken piano lessons, but that didn't stick for me. It was too individual. And not sexy enough. Nobody ever talks about "giving the piano player some." Some love. I'm referring to *love*. [Narrator: *That was for Will's mom. He knows that, even if nobody else does, she is going to read this book.*] Anyway, I wanted to be in a band.

Now that I have children, I can't imagine how exasperating it must have been for my parents to raise me. Growing up, I was the kid who wanted to try everything. They were constantly shuttling me back and forth to one of the 3,304 activities I signed up for. They drove me back and forth to practice when I told them I wanted to play basketball, then football, then baseball. I'd tell them that I had signed up for a speech competition. "That's great!" they'd say, then I'd tell them it was tomorrow. In a city forty-five minutes away. And I needed a ride. And a new tie.

The way I see it, that was my parents' fault for instilling an incredible dose of self-esteem at an early age. You can't tell a child to believe that he can do anything he puts his mind to and then expect him not to put his mind to everything. So, when my fifth-grade teacher asked the class who wanted to be in the band, of course I raised my hand and chose the trumpet.

That seemed like the next best thing to the drums. Trumpeters could be sexy. I mean, look at Miles Davis. Does he look like someone that didn't get a lot of . . . love? As usual, my parents supported my pursuit of becoming a musical prodigy. Especially my dad. He was bursting with pride and revealed that I had unknowingly followed in his footsteps. Apparently, he had also been a trumpet player when he was in grade school. After I told him, he disappeared for a few moments and returned with a very important, very special gift. A well-worn trumpet. The exact same one he played as a kid. Wow. (This must've been how Jesus felt when Joseph gave him his first carpentry belt.) I was overjoyed to receive that trumpet. He was handing down something really important to me. The first time he had ever done that. It was a cool, magical moment.

On the first day of band practice, I strutted into the band room with my dad's prized Packer family trumpet in hand. I felt like a Targaryen with a dragon egg. Until I looked around the room and witnessed my primarily white bandmates brandishing brand-new trombones and saxophones that shimmered under the fluorescent lights. Wait, everybody got new instruments for band? *Everybody?* These things were flawless and golden. They looked like they might play music by themselves. I looked down at my Packer trumpet and all of a sudden it looked tarnished and dull. I had never noticed how many dents and scratches it had on it. Never mind that it was over twenty-five years old. It suddenly looked a hundred. Like the first trumpet ever made.

I stood out like a sore thumb. I was embarrassed. It felt like all the other kids were laughing at me, like, "Where'd you get *that* thing?" A cute girl I kind of liked tried to defend me. "Stop it, guys. It's the first day of band. He probably hasn't had a chance to get his new trumpet yet. Right?" Ummm, right. All the magic went out the window.

Now, I distinctly remember going home that night and trying to figure out the exact approach to ask my dad for a new trumpet. I remember being afraid that I might hurt his feelings. He loved that old trumpet and was so proud that I would be playing it. I couldn't figure out what to say and decided that he was just gonna have to get over it because there was *no way* I was going back to catch more flack from the band kids. I decided it would be best just to beg like my life depended on it. And beg I did. "*Plllleeeeeaaaasssse* get me a new trumpet, Dad. *Please!*"

I was so ready for a *Titanic*-sized disappointment from my old man, but you know what? He wasn't even fazed. In fact, it was like he expected it. I remember he said to me very calmly, "Remember how fortunate you felt to have that trumpet this summer before school started? Remember how you were so happy to have any instrument at all? Remember how you were so excited to even be able to play in the band? You've allowed those kids to take that joy away from you. If you really, really want, I'll get you a new trumpet, but be clear this is you falling victim to outward perception. Which you should never do."

Dang. That hit me right in the ego. He was right, of course. I had let the opinions of others cloud my judgment. I forgot that it wasn't about the trumpet's appearance, but about the music we made with it. I had lost sight of the joy of playing, being a part of the band, the privilege I had to have any trumpet at all, and became fixated on shiny objects. His words hit me deep. I took the time to really process what he said and think about the symbolism behind his words. And then exactly 2.3 seconds later my little spoiled ass said, "Yep. I *gotta* have a new trumpet."

I mean valor, integrity, and self-assuredness is good and all, but I wanted to fit in, you know? We're all guilty of falling victim to the approvals, judgments, and perspectives of other people. Why? These people don't really matter in the greater scheme of things. *Your* approval, judgment, and perspective is what really matters. Why do you care what someone who is not you thinks? We need to get over that.

My dad, being the loving and understanding guy he is, got me that new trumpet. And he never missed a band performance that school year. Then he didn't even say anything the following year when I left band and moved on to the next extracurricular thing that caught my eye. Looking back on that whole debacle, it taught me a valuable lesson. We often get caught up in appearances and what others think of us. We forget that it's not about the shiny exterior but the heart and soul we put into our passions. It's about making music, both literally and metaphorically, in a way that brings us joy and fulfillment.

More than that, if I was in a concert, who is the audience more likely to remember? The towheads with identical instruments or the little Black kid playing his heart out with the beat-up trumpet? It's way more interesting to be the guy or girl who stands out in the crowd. Ask Miles Davis . . . he got *all* the love.

14

Put a Check with a Check with a Check

You Did a Thing. Good for You. Now Keep Going.

I consider myself to be pretty cultured and intellectual. College grad with honors. Astute reasoning capabilities. Solid oratory skills. But when it comes to my go-to music, give me southern, vulgar rap for $500, Alex. The more imprudent the better, honestly. It's the energy, the culture, and the hidden life lessons within the lyrics that do it for me.

A great example is "Just Like Candy" by 8Ball & MJG, a hood classic and a Memphis, Tennessee, ode to the shiny paint job on a car. For the uninitiated, "candy" paint is a reference to transparent paint applied over a highly reflective, brightly colored base coat, giving it a hard candy–type look. In the song, MJG tells the listener if you want to get a dope paint job like me, "You need to put a check with a check with a check." Meaning to afford a look as fly as his you gotta make some money, and then some more money, and then, you guessed it, some more money after that. Now, for me, that lyric was never about shiny paint jobs. I've never had "candy" paint in my life and never wanted it. Okay, that's not true. In high school I desperately wanted a fly paint job on my car. I might have gotten one if, as you might recall, my good friend hadn't stolen my car as retribution for perceived betrayal.

To me, that lyric means you can't just have one success. You can't just have one goal you accomplish. You can't just have two goals that you accomplish. You gotta put a success with a success with a success. Once you've achieved some success, *keep going*!

Opening weekend for a theatrical movie is nerve-racking. As I mentioned, it's literally like waiting for election returns on a November Tuesday. As the film's producer, I begin to get hourly updates of box-office numbers at noon on that Friday. Now, this is noon Eastern Standard Time, and usually only a few theaters are reporting by then. But based on the decades of data that Hollywood analysts who track such things have, they will extrapolate projections for the entire weekend based on the midday matinee gross of a couple theaters in Manhattan. Then another batch of numbers comes in at one P.M., then two P.M., and so on. It's crazy-making because you want to look away but you just can't. And with every hour the projections for the all-important opening weekend continue to update.

I will never forget the *Ride Along* opening weekend. Every hour the projections kept growing and growing. People were *loving* our action buddy comedy starring Ice Cube and Kevin Hart and turning out in droves to see it. By the time Sunday rolled around, it was the highest-grossing movie on Martin Luther King, Jr., weekend ever! It was the biggest opening of my career by far.

That weekend we felt like the kings of the world. We had worked very, very hard, and it had paid off. I had taken Cube and Kev on a cross-country promotional tour à la my first indie theatrical release *Trois*. This time, instead of driving back roads and staying in Motel 6s, it was private jets and high-end hotels, but the grind was still a grind. Coming off that historic opening for the movie, a bunch of the actors and crew wanted to celebrate. "Vegas!" it was suggested. "Let's *go*!" I said enthusiastically.

Now, it just so happened I had another movie starring Kevin Hart that was set to release one month later. It was called *About Last Night,* and because the dates were so close, that Sunday of *Ride Along*'s triumphant release we were scheduled to do a promotional shoot with Kev and other actors from *About Last Night.*

I went to Kev and told him that the crew was going to Vegas and that I knew we had the shoot for *About Last Night,* but I could try to find some other time to do it so we could turn all the way up that weekend. His response surprised me. Kevin goes, "Let me tell you something, Will Packer. I've been here before. Vegas will always be there. You know what's better than one hit? Two hits. Let's put this work in. Forget Vegas." Wow. Ummm, okay, Kev. What zombie had invaded the body of the same guy who almost murdered my career with Carmelo Anthony in a New York nightclub? Let's skip Vegas and put the work in. Yeah, that's exactly what I was thinking. *{Narrator: That's not at all what Will Packer was thinking.}*

It was around that time that Kevin told me a story about a tough year he had—projects getting canceled, stand-up not doing well. He didn't make much money at all. Then the following year he finally had a big year; let's say he made $250,000. He promised himself he'd be really smart about it. Save $75K and enjoy the other $175,000. At the end of the year, his accountant says, "I have great news."

And Kevin's like, "Yeah, I bet you do!" fully prepared to have to use the $75K he had put away.

The accountant's like, "Yep, you had a great year. Now you've got some money to make up for the past few years of taxes you missed. You only owe a half million dollars in back taxes!" Kev told me he promised himself if he ever got a chance at real success he wouldn't let anything stand in his way.

So instead of going to Vegas we put in the work of shooting the promo for *About Last Night,* which became another hit a month later. In fact, that year, 2014, was a monster one for me. I released *four* movies in one year and *three* of them opened number one at the box office. I couldn't have done that with a bunch of (albeit well-earned) Vegas partying.

Kevin Hart had that "check with a check with a check" mentality. Not only is he one of my best friends in the business, he's also somebody who's an inspiration to me because he's had it, lost it, and worked hard to get it back again. And he works *very* hard. I mean, to his credit, even the *Ride Along*/Madison Square Garden near disaster was Kevin trying to work *too* hard and complete a movie *and* stand-up special at the same damn time. I've definitely adopted that perpetual-grind mentality. After a big success, I always come back to triumph and disaster. Don't get too high. Don't get too low. Keep an even keel. Keep working, keep grinding.

Put a check with a check with a check.

If you've ever succeeded at anything, you know how incredible it feels. You put in all that work and all that effort to have that success, but you didn't put in all that work and effort to just have that *one* success. You put it in so you could have multiple successes. Maybe so you can have a lifetime of success. Maybe so you can create a lasting legacy of successes. Maybe you did it for your kids, or your career, or your community. You went in and busted your tail to get there, so take full advantage of it. It sounds counterintuitive, but working hard gives you the benefit of being able to work harder.

Don't let the volume of work get you down. Remember, having the work means you've worked hard enough to be that busy. Let the work be the privilege. As I write this, I had ten video conference meetings today. By the seventh one my head was spinning. By the tenth I was speaking Swahili, and I don't know Swahili. But when I thought about complaining I said to myself, "If I was not Will

Packer at the level I'm at, nobody would want to meet with me at all. I'm so fortunate."

The work I put in allows me the benefit of putting in more work and having more successes. I no longer think, "Oh, we won. That was the goal. I accomplished it. It's over." In that *Ride Along* situation, we had an opportunity to go have another victory. And Kev said, "You think it's great to have one number one this year? How would you feel if you had two number ones this year?" I ended up with three.

Don't get complacent in your success. There'll be time to celebrate later. The most successful people I know are never satisfied. Legendary Tampa Bay Buccaneers (and a few years with some other team) quarterback Tom Brady always said his favorite ring is his next one. The most successful people have that mentality.

I'm not telling you to never, ever feel accomplished. I'm not telling you to never, ever be happy with your achievements. I'm not telling you to never, ever celebrate your success. And I'm certainly not telling you not to balance all that hard work with harder play. What I'm telling you is to not be satisfied. Satisfaction sounds like satiation. Being satiated means you're full. You no longer want to eat. You gorged at the buffet, and now you just want to go to sleep and let the carbs do their work. No! Don't be that person. Stay hungry. Even as you celebrate your success, be looking toward the next success. "Vegas" will be there. Crank some hood southern rap all the way up and keep grinding. Hard. Just like candy.

STAY IN THE LAB

It's the work we put in when no one is watching that makes everybody pay attention later! We've all fallen victim to being captivated by the end results we witness, often overlooking the behind-the-scenes work that led to those achievements. This lesson became evident to me during a memorable trip to Miami with my friend 69, whose real name is Derrell Fields. Police officer Derrell Fields, to be exact. He's not just my friend, he's my best friend. He's also not actually six foot nine, he's six foot ten. But according to him, 69 just sounds cooler. *[Narrator: For clarity, it's pronounced Six Nine, not Sixty-Nine, which would be an even weirder nickname.]*

Anyway, 69 and I found ourselves amid a vibrant pool party, surrounded by people with chiseled physiques and impeccable bodies. I looked down at my own very much not chiseled or impeccable body. In that moment, I was inspired to transform my own physique before our next visit to South Beach in a couple months. I proclaimed, "When we come back I'mma be ripped. I'm about to get serious!" But Six challenged my mindset and revealed a profound truth.

"No, you ain't," he responded, shattering my aspirations.

"You're just a hater, bruh. I'll show you," I snapped. He explained that it had nothing to do with me or my work ethic, but the fact that those individuals with remarkable bodies had started their fitness journeys loooong before. The bodies they showcased were a result of the work they had put in during the previous *years*, not a sudden transformation months before our return.

"Summer bodies are made the summer before," he said. Of course he was right.

I started to think about how true success, whether it's achieving a fit physique or excelling in any endeavor, requires consistent effort and long-term dedication. We often underestimate the value of putting in the work behind closed doors, away from the prying eyes of the world. It is during these moments in the "lab" that our true transformation occurs.

The key lies in understanding that the work we put in when

nobody is watching is what sets the stage for everyone to take notice later. It's in those quiet moments of self-discipline and unwavering commitment that our dreams and aspirations begin to take shape. The lab becomes our sanctuary, where we can experiment, grow, and refine our craft.

But because we live in a world of immediate gratification and immediate results, we all feel the need to let everybody into our personal "labs." If we're not showing results and progress, then it must not be happening. "Pics or it didn't happen" is a common social media sentiment.

Forget that. Embrace the power of consistent effort, even when the world remains oblivious to your journey. Be driven by the understanding that your success is not determined solely by the attention and applause we receive in the present. Instead, it is forged by the dedication we demonstrate when nobody is watching. The lab becomes our training ground, our platform for growth and self-improvement. It is in this sacred space that we cultivate the skills, knowledge, and resilience necessary to reach our goals. We must persevere, knowing that the sweat, sacrifices, and unyielding passion we invest will ultimately yield the results we desire.

Remember the next time you're admiring amazing summer bodies that they were crafted in the previous summers. Away from the public gaze. You're only seeing them now because they're ready to be unveiled. Likewise, our accomplishments are a reflection of the consistent work we put in when nobody is watching. So, go forth and commit to your journey in the lab, knowing that one day, the world will pay attention to the remarkable transformation that occurred behind the scenes. Meanwhile, I'm still working on my abs, and 69 is still hating.

15

Riding, Dying, and Selling Oranges

Find Your Secret Weapon

You may have seen the Internet meme: *You want a ride or die, but you also want somebody to ask questions. Like, "Where are we riding to and why we gotta die?"*

I one hundred percent agree. You want somebody who will have your back and be loyal through the tough times no matter what, right? But you don't want somebody to just blindly ride or die and not tell you, "We're going a hundred and ten, there's a hairpin turn coming up, you're three shots of vodka in, so slam on the damn brakes!" You want that person. I know *ride or die within reason* doesn't have the same ring to it but that's what you want.

You need a Shayla.

Shayla P. Cowan started as my executive assistant and rose through the ranks of my company to become chief of staff and then launch our Collective Edge Management division. Shayla Cowan is not just a valuable person in my life, she is my secret weapon. In our industry, everyone is focused on titles and positions. They want to meet the big shots, the presidents, the CEOs, the heads of marketing and distribution and film production. I'm that big shot to a lot of folks. A lot of them are trying to get to me. But let me tell you who truly has my ear: Shayla. As my executive assistant, she was my trusted adviser and her opinion weighed heavily in my decisions. Yet, despite her immense value, people would often overlook her. They would skip over her and try to go straight to me, thinking that I was the one solely making the decisions. But I knew better. I knew that Shayla was one of the crucial keys to my success. One of the best ways to judge someone is how they treat people who they perceive can't offer them anything. *{Narrator: Read that last line again. That was a bar.}* That's something I learned early on in my career—to be savvy and find the Shayla in every person's life.

Titles don't tell the whole story when it comes to influence and power. Sure, everyone wants to get to the top dogs, but it's the people they trust and rely on who truly hold the keys to success.

You might not ever meet a Fortune 500 CEO, but I guarantee you that he or she has a version of an executive assistant/consultant/right hand/confidant that they entrust with a lot of authority. They may not have fancy titles, but they have the power to change your life and your career. So, if you can't get an audience with the big boss who has the power to green-light your project, finance your endeavor, or hire you for the dream position, find their *right hand.* Your success depends on it.

One of my executives once jokingly commented that I thought Shayla was infallible and that I never disagreed with her. I explained how that couldn't be further from the truth. I disagree with Shayla all the time. People who are really successful over long periods of time know they need to have people around them who have differing perspectives and aren't afraid to express them. I told my exec that while I don't always see eye to eye with Shayla, I never question her loyalty or drive. I know that no matter what happens, she has my back. That gives me a great deal of confidence.

I asked him, "What if all my financing dried up, I became persona non grata in the film industry and was left with no options at all?" I said, "If I had to shutter this company and let everyone go, you and the other execs would start polishing your résumés and making calls. Thanks to your time at this company, you've got proven track records in the notoriously fickle film industry, and most of you would have no trouble finding employment. But what if I, on the other hand, was reduced to selling oranges on the side of the road under a freeway overpass? What would you do?"

He said, "Well, I can't imagine that ever happening, but I guess I would try to get you a job at my new company."

I said, "And I appreciate that. Truly."

But the difference is I asked Shayla the same question and she didn't even have to contemplate an answer. There was no hypothetical plan B. She shrugged and responded quickly: "Which underpass would we be working under?" That's why Shayla will always be an essential part of my crew. While everyone else is uploading their CVs to LinkedIn, Shayla would be on her way to find some oranges.

I'm successful. I get a lot of props and publicity for my success, but I couldn't do it without the team around me. And at the core of that team is someone whose loyalty is unquestioned. So my advice to you guys is to get yourself a Shayla. A rock.

As a leader you need to put a bunch of smart and capable people around you and listen to all of them. Hear their opinions and perspectives. Question them and push back. But the true key to your success is having people around you whose motivations and intentions you never have to question. That's very, very important. You don't need a big team; you just need the right one. Prioritize the traits of loyalty and work ethic when evaluating talent. And make sure your team feels appreciated and seen so you can retain them, because those folks are very hard to come by.

Of course, the inverse of this principle is also true. Loyalty alone doesn't mean someone should be on your orange-selling team.

Too often we doom our careers, goals, and dreams to failure by saddling them with the burden of relationships that are based on nothing except time and comfort. The length of a relationship doesn't always correlate to its quality. Just because you're still close with someone you sat behind in the third grade doesn't mean you share the same values or vision or work ethic. I have a good friend who just happens to be a professional football player. One day we were out together (you know how we high-level athletes get down) and my dude was unloading about how his childhood friends, his "day ones," were holding him back. And even though he had already helped them for years, he still felt obligated to them.

I told him he shouldn't feel an obligation to people who've always been around him who aren't making him better. People underestimate the influence, good and bad, of the company you keep. One of my mantras is "If you see yourself as an eagle but you're hanging with ducks, when you open your mouth, all other people hear is a quack." If you're the best, most successful, hardest-working person in your circle, you need a new circle, because your circle is not pushing you to be better.

You shouldn't be carrying anybody who's simply from your past. Are you even that person anymore? If there are people who are no longer fitting the phase in your life that you're in, be unapologetic and move on. Don't risk your success because you don't want to hurt somebody's feelings. We all evolve and change. If you're not evolving and changing, what are you doing?

I think one thing I'd add to that is that "sphere of influence" applies to all of us. It's something that when we hear it, we think we're talking about world leaders and people who have access to the nuclear codes or Donald Trump's hair gel. We all exert influence over others and operate within their sphere of influence. And we need to be conscious of whether our sphere is bringing us down or elevating us. Don't underestimate the impact of those closest to you.

Be honest with yourself about whether their influence is positive or negative.

You want to keep people around you who are positive, but not overly so, not sycophantic, but people who push you to be better and who bring out the best you. And, of course, who know how to find cheap oranges.

IDENTIFYING THE IT FACTOR

Some people would say I have an eye for talent. *[Narrator: Will is "some people."]* It's been true with Shayla Cowan and Tiffany Haddish. I put Kevin Hart in the movie that really broke him out as a movie star. I put Idris Elba in his first theatrical feature, *The Gospel*. Today, Idris and I have done six movies together and counting. Regé-Jean Page was in my production of *Roots* before he blew up in *Bridgerton*. I helped make *Little* star Marsai Martin the youngest executive producer in Hollywood history.

I stack my casts and company with the best and brightest. I didn't create the talent that these people have, but I was a conduit for their success. Point is, you yourself don't always have to be singularly talented in a particular way in order to spot and nurture talent. You don't have to be the smartest, fastest, or strongest, but if you surround yourself with the smartest, fastest, and strongest, you're going to win.

Steve Jobs was not a programmer or a coder. That's not what he did. He was an innovator and a visionary—unlike, say, Bill Gates, who really was a coder. Bill was amazingly talented in that specific area. You may not be a prodigy in a particular field yourself, but you can be a Will Packer or even a Steve Jobs for that matter. You can be an innovator. You can be somebody who surrounds themself with talented people. That's what I did with

Idris and Kevin and Tiffany. I had a platform that allowed them to utilize the talents that they already had. Sometimes it's about lining up the right talent with the right platform and the right moment in time. Working on your skill of identifying good people is time well spent. Hone your instincts, then trust them.

16

In Praise of Praise

The Snowball Effect of Validation

I had a high school football coach named Mark Wizowaty, affection-ately referred to as "Coach Wiz." First of all, yes, I played high school football. Second of all, it's none of your business how good I was. I was on the team. In Florida! That's like all we do. Okay, that's not true, Floridians actually do a bunch of headline-grabbing things, but in between dodging neighborhood-eating sinkholes and wrestling alligators that crawl out of our toilets, we play football . . . and we play it well.

Now, our team wasn't the greatest, and by that I mean we sucked. *But* we played much better than we should have, which is to say we would've sucked much more if it wasn't for our coach.

Wizowaty was a natural leader of almost-men. Or maybe he read a manual. Not sure. In any case, Coach Wiz was never under the impression that he was going to lead us to gridiron glory. Despite his name, he was not a coaching wizard who found fame under Florida's Friday-night lights. In a state bursting at the seams with uncut athletic diamonds, Coach Wiz worked in a coal mine. Compared to our rivals, St. Petersburg High was undersized and less talented, but Wiz managed to squeeze every ounce of ability out of his players.

The genius of Coach Wiz was that he made every single player, from the stars to the benchwarmers, feel like they were essential to the team. He had a gravelly I-smoke-five-packs-for-breakfast voice (although, weirdly, I never saw him smoke), and I remember him saying, "Packer, I see you out there. You're smaller and that makes people underestimate you. But not me. I know that you've got something inside you that most people can't see, that makes you bigger than the biggest guys on the field. That's your heart. You keep working and trying hard to accomplish the physical things and let that big ol' heart of yours do the rest."

I was like five foot five and weighed 125 pounds, in my football uniform, drenched, with rocks in my pockets. I might not have been the second coming of Deion Sanders, but I was quick, fearless, and had pretty good hands. I was also one of Coach Wiz's favorites. Wiz never told me this personally, but I could tell. I'm sure he didn't announce it so as not to appear biased. *{Narrator: Yeah, I'm sure that was it.}* I'm pretty sure he put me on the second team because Coach Wiz knew that, unlike those fragile, faster, more talented players who started, my ego could handle it. He would often come up to me after practice and say, "You're giving your all. You're doing your thing. Keep it up. I'm watching. Don't give up. Don't stop working hard."

That was enough for me. I was always willing to work hard, give effort, and apply the lessons of one of the first-rate coaches in all of second-rate high school football. I would've run through a wall for Coach Wiz. And I did. I was not afraid to go flying headfirst into two-hundred-pound Leon Lett types. In fact, I still have a bad neck and back to this day. I didn't say I was smart. I said I was fearless.

Not only did Coach's belief in me inspire me to work even

harder, but it made me not want to let him down. I wanted *him* to win. I felt like our successes were tied to each other. And that's exactly how you want someone on your team to feel.

Every player on the team felt like they were Wiz's favorite. He would give a version of that same speech to every player and tailor it so that it fit them. But the fact that he took the time to say it to a second-string cornerback tells you the type of coach he was.

Unfortunately, our team simply didn't have the talent to compete with the other insanely talented Florida teams. But we played hard. We even made the playoffs one year. None of your business whether I played in that game or not. Somebody had to keep an eye out for the alligators.

In 1998, I graduated from college and was prepared to take Hollywood by storm. For some reason, Hollywood wasn't beating down my door even after the success of my blockbuster college film, *Chocolate City* (when I say *blockbuster* I mean it was in Blockbuster video stores), so I jumped at the chance to intern on *Ride,* the film produced by Reginald and Warrington Hudlin.

Ride was about a bus full of aspiring entertainers riding to Miami to make a music video. It had stars like Lady of Rage, Downtown Julie Brown, and a little-known thespian who went by the name Snoop Dogg. *{Narrator: It was also destined to be a Blockbuster hit.}*

Now, in contrast to Coach Wiz, my boss on the movie gave me zero praise. The second we wrapped for the day, I had to immediately place a very specific drink in his hands—exactly two parts gin, one part tonic, on ice. I could not be late.

This person didn't care that I made *Chocolate City,* nor did he care that there was a former Student Supreme Court chief justice in his department. I went from big man on campus to the low man on the totem pole. My job was basically to get coffee for my department and untangle cable cords. There was nobody lower than me. The PAs told me what to do. I was at the bottom, and there were people on that set who a thousand percent treated me like I was the bottom. Some would yell at me, "Move! You're in the way!" if I was standing in the wrong place because I had never been on a Hollywood movie set before. But those folks didn't care. I meant nothing to them. I was a nobody.

On the other hand, there were also people on that set, including the Hudlin brothers themselves, who treated me with respect, who treated me like I was a young aspiring filmmaker who someday might become something. That made me work so much harder. I don't want to brag, so I say this with all humility: Everyone on set knew I was the absolute best intern. *{Narrator: That's literally zero humility.}* My cable was never tangled. I always brought extra napkins, straws, and creamer with the coffee without being asked. I always put a lime in the gin and tonic; mixologist Packer on the case! And because I pioneered a groundbreaking new technique where I would wrap napkins around the coffee cup as insulation (for some reason we were constantly out of those little insulator sleeve things), I swear my coffee was eight degrees hotter than the other interns'. The Hudlins recognized my contributions, and because they gave me encouraging pats on the back, it made me want to go above and beyond on the mundane tasks that were my responsibility. I recognized that positive reinforcement technique immediately.

You never forget how people make you feel. Flash forward two decades—now that I'm Will Packer, super producer with the ability to hire full film crews, nearly everybody on that set has asked me for a job in one way or another. And guess what? I remember those people who treated me with respect. I remember those who shunned me. Ain't no fun when the rabbit got the gun.

When I'm on a set now and I see that kid who is running around, scrambling, hustling their butt off as the lowest on the totem pole, I always try to take some time to go over, shake their hand, and say, "Hey, I was you." When I have somebody on my team who shows leadership, I have found that it's not enough to just give positive reinforcement. I will go overboard to try to make people feel like "I'm being noticed. I got this. I can do this!"

If someone gives their full effort and delivers what amounts to an eight out of ten, shower them with praise. The next time they will give you a nine. It's like when somebody says, "Hey, have you been working out?" Even if you really haven't but you're having a good-fitting-clothes day and somebody notices, it feels good. The next time you're in the gym you'll be treadmilling like crazy, sweating your tail off in response to that positive reinforcement. It's good to hear and you want to earn more. That's the snowball effect of validation. Use that to your benefit when you're trying to get your team/peers/co-workers to row in the same direction.

Prioritizing praising my team is one of the keys to my *own* success. You may be shocked to learn that I'm a much better producer than I was a football player. Whether you're building a small business, leading a fundraiser, or working as the CEO of a multinational corporation, showering someone who works with, for, or alongside you with sincere praise more times than not inspires them to put in even more effort. And when they win, the team wins; and when the team wins, you win.

17

Go Ahead, Make Another Me

Don't Let People Steal Your Power

As you strive to attain the lofty goals you've set for yourself, it's important to be prepared for when you actually start to reach those goals. When you make it to or near "the top" (however you're defining it), people will try to claim your success. I personally know this to be true. That is not me whining; that is a fact. I have had several people close to me, including one family member, brag that they "made" me. In one instance, someone I know well who had very little involvement with my career was trying to get into the movie business. This person actually had the audacity to pitch a studio executive at Sony Pictures with this gem: "You saw what I did with Will Packer. I'm a kingmaker." Umm, excuse me?!

One of my favorite songs is Jay-Z's "Lost One," which is in part about the aftermath of a professional breakup, when a former business partner claimed to be responsible for his stratospheric success. Jay doesn't name names, but he doesn't have to. Jay-Z simply responds, "I heard [MFers] saying they made Hov, . . . Okay, so make another Hov." It's kinda perfect. You made me, huh? Instead of pointing out how idiotic that sounds, you know what? Go ahead and make another me.

"I owe a lot of my success to a lot of people," Jay-Z explained about the lyrics, "but ultimately, no one made me. This is the kind of lie that people get told all the time, sometimes in romantic relationships, sometimes in their professional lives. That somehow who they are is a result of other people's investment in them. It's vital to resist that or you risk losing yourself."

That lyric reminds me every day: Don't let people steal your power. I tell my kids that all the time. My daughters especially. I say to them, make no mistake, in all relationships—business, personal, doesn't matter—*you* are the prize. Never give that power away, and never let anybody forget that you are the prize.

Once you get to certain levels of success, things will change. The number of people around you will increase. The type of attention you get will be different. Not everyone will have great intentions. Some will want to leech your power, your money, your limelight. Many will claim to have known you when, and they may have. They may have even been instrumental in your ascent. But make no mistake: Your success is just that—*your* success. Nobody can be you. Nobody can replicate exactly what you did and how you did it, and that's what the line "Go on, make another me" is about.

It's like when you try to copy a recipe from your favorite restaurant. You can come close, but it'll never be identical because the restaurant gets their meat from a certain purveyor, they use a specific kind of butter in their sauces, they have a Michelin-rated chef that uses a pan that costs $1,000. Your little Walmart pan and corner-store sauces just aren't the same. Your journey is entirely your own and nobody can duplicate it, as hard as they might try. You have your own special sauce.

Not to say that you reach your goals alone. Of course you have help. And not giving your supporters any credit is disrespectful too. Be gracious and be thankful. But remember, it would not have happened without the most important element, and that's you. Don't be so gracious that you give somebody else your power. Because people will take it if you let them.

Everybody wants credit. We are in a credit-obsessed society. That is all we care about. "I just want people to know I did it. Whatever *it* is. I want my name on it. And I want my name at the top. Unless it's bad, then I want nothing to do with it. I'll sue you if you try to put my name on it." In Hollywood, 90 percent of the final sticking points in negotiations revolve around credit. I kid you not, megamillion-dollar deals are on the verge of falling apart all the time around credit and positioning and font size and typeface. {*Narrator: By the way, Will's exact requirements are "Credit in main titles, on a separate card, in first position of all 'produced by' credits." He's one to talk.*} Everybody fights, fights, fights for their credit. With that being said, knowing that we live in a credit-obsessed society, it doesn't mean that you shouldn't get credit where credit is due, or that you shouldn't fight for your credit when it's owed. However, sometimes people become so focused on the credit, they lose sight of the bigger picture. They lose focus on what really matters: the work, the execution, the ultimate goal of getting the project done in the best way possible.

President Harry S. Truman once said, "It's amazing what you can accomplish if you do not care who gets the credit." Mind you, this is coming from the dude who dropped the atomic bomb, so I get why he doesn't want ownership on that one. But the reality is, that quote is true. If we all just focused on the work and not whose name is going to be where, imagine the results.

I'm not going to lie, at first it definitely irked me that my "friend" claimed my success to try to get a deal with Sony. But you know what I told the executive? "Tell them to do it again," I laughed. By the way, I laugh that same laugh whenever fans/filmmakers/critics tell me what I did wrong on one of my hit movies. I laugh *really* hard when it's one of my number-one movies. Doesn't mean the criticism isn't valid. Just means, to me, it sure is funny.

There's a great scene in Oliver Stone's iconic football film *Any Given Sunday.* The veteran coach, played by Al Pacino, is arguing with the young new owner, played by Cameron Diaz, who inherited the team from her father. Her dad and the coach won five Pantheon Cups together, the equivalent of the Super Bowl. Despite that, the new owner is trying to shake things up. Their fight goes a little something like this:

"Your dad would never do it this way."

"My dad's dead. It's *my* team now."

"You know what? Go win a Pantheon Cup."

"I know I don't have five Pantheon Cups but . . ."

"No, no, no, just go win *one.*"

That is the mantra I have in my head when someone tries to leech on to my success. You don't have to produce *ten* movies that open at number one. Start with just one. Good luck.

IF IT AIN'T BROKE . . .

If you are able to make it to a certain level where people want to glom on to your success, undoubtedly you got there by doing something well. And probably doing that thing repeatedly.

When I first moved to Atlanta, nothing much was happening for Rob Hardy and me. We were trying to get our production company off the ground and mostly failing at it. We were beating our heads against the Hollywood wall. Many of our friends, recent college grads like us, were making high five/low six figures, driving new cars, and enjoying all entry-level corporate America had to offer. I was answering phones, doing data entry, and delivering newspapers. Rob, for some unknown reason, was cold-selling overpriced vacuum cleaners and gourmet cutlery door-to-door. In order to not go crazy partying and carousing every night, we needed to put our young restless energy into something positive. We'd go to the legendary Atlanta hotspot Uptown Comedy Corner and watch open mic night because it was free to get in. The amateurs up there did not slay. It was uncomfortable to watch. "Yo, these people are terrible," I whispered to Rob. "I can do that way better."

"If you do it, I'll do it," Rob whispered back. "But you gotta go first."

Anyone who knows anything about stand-up knows where this is heading . . .

Now, here's something that you must understand. White comedy clubs and Black comedy clubs are like the United States and England. You think we're speaking the same language, but once you go over there, oh no, different worlds. In a white comedy club, even if you're not funny, you may still get a few polite sympathy chuckles from the audience. The host will come up afterward and say, "Give it up again for Emmanuel. He's still learning; show him some love." At a Black comedy club, the host goes onstage beforehand and says, "Look, y'all have a job to do. Your job is to let these up-and-comers know that they are not good. That's your job as an audience to set them right. If you don't do your job, then these amateurs may think they are actually good when they leave here. Then they are going to fail and have a miserable life and it will be all your fault. So, when they get up here, if these people are not the best comics you ever heard in your life, boo their asses. Now, let's practice, everybody. One, two, three, booooooooo!"

I went up on a Sunday night, the fourth person to go. Rob gave me an encouraging fist bump and a "You got this, bruh" and then sat in the audience to cheer me on. The first three amateurs all got booed mercilessly. I'm not a shy guy, but I was nervous. I had my little routine, I practiced it, I had my beginner jokes ready to go. Miraculously, I did not get booed. I wish I could say I slayed, but I didn't write this book to tell you lies. I wasn't that great. But I was charismatic, I had stage presence, and my jokes didn't suck, so that was enough to make me the best of a bad bunch that night. A renowned Atlanta comedian who has since passed, named Nard, came up to me after the show and said, "You got something, man. If you really want to do this, keep working it to get a little bit better. You're obviously a novice, but you got something there."

The next open mic night was two days later. On Tuesday, both Rob and I went back to the club. I was going up again and this time Rob had to go up too. That was the deal. I had written up an entirely new routine because it was the same club and I didn't want to come off as stale. I was now an experienced stand-up with open mic pedigree and a blessing from Nard under my belt, so before the show, I felt qualified to tell Rob, "Listen, if they don't laugh at a joke, whatever you do, just keep going. Don't stop. You got this, bruh. I'll be cheering for you."

Rob went first and told his first joke and it was crickets. Not even a boo. He kept going and the silence was deafening. But like I told him to, he didn't pause, he didn't hesitate. He just kept going. Because of my advice, the crowd didn't understand where one joke ended and the other began. They were waiting for any punch line at all and just thought he was telling one long story. When he was on like his fifth joke, a drunk lady in the front yelled out, "This [MFer] ain't telling no jokes! This is just a long dumbass story!" That's all it took. The whole crowd erupted.

BOOOOOOOOOOOOOOOO!

What happened next is one of the least proud moments in my life. You have to understand, Rob was my best friend in the entire world. Fraternity brothers, business partners, roommates, all of it. He got off the stage and slunk to the back of the club, where I was waiting to go on next. He sat next to me after getting booed. You could tell he felt awful. "That was kinda rough, huh?" he sighed, shaking his head, and then he looked to me for any sign of encouragement whatsoever.

I am utterly ashamed to say I literally turned my back on Rob and acted as if I. Did. Not. Know. Him. I was so nervous after seeing him crash and burn that I didn't even want the association. I was afraid the bad mojo might be contagious. This man had just gotten booed offstage, and he came down and was trying to talk to his dear friend. He tried to touch my shoulder and I literally scooted away like "Don't get any of that on me." I'm telling you I denied him like Peter did Jesus. Shameful. And God saw it too. I soon learned that karma is undefeated and God don't like ugly.

I hopped up onstage next, but I wasn't nearly as confident as I was the first time. I told a joke about how teachers tell kids not to run with scissors. "That's the dumbest thing ever," I said. "Have you ever looked at those safety scissors you have in elementary school? You could try to kill yourself with those scissors and it wouldn't work." Then I pretended to slit my own throat with safety scissors.

BOOOOOOOOOOOO! I didn't even get to a second joke.

There are two lessons here. One is how it was all Rob's fault because he got the crowd all riled up and ready to boo, so I didn't stand a chance. [Narrator: It was definitely not Rob's fault.]

The other is that Nard came up to me afterward and cried, "Dude, what the hell? Why did you change your routine? What was that? What was that new joke?"

"I can't do the same jokes . . ."

"Yeah, yeah you can," he interrupted immediately. My new mentor was so disappointed. "You had something that worked two nights ago. You think these are the same people? Once you have something that works, you keep it!"

It had never occurred to me until that moment that even the

best comedians repeat their routines over and over and over again. Because what works, works. Audiences will often go see their favorite comedians and wait specifically for their favorite bits that they've heard a hundred times before. Elbowing the person next to them like, "Wait till he does the scissors bit!"

Lesson learned. When you get in a good groove, you stick with it. Don't feel the need to switch it up. If you got something and it's working, it's okay to keep doing it until the audience or market changes. As long as you still feel fulfilled by it. Some of the most successful people in the world have perfected doing one thing really, really well.

In the meantime, I'm still working on fine-tuning the perfect fifteen-minute stand-up set. Wait till you see it. It *kills* at white comedy clubs.

18

The Art of the Sale

Always Be Selling

Life is about sales. Whether you realize it or not, you've been selling yourself in some form or fashion since the day you were born, and you'll continue having to sell yourself one way or another until the day you die. Before you get depressed about you at age ninety-nine in a soiled pair of Depends, looking for your teeth so you can convince your caretaker that you are worthy, let me allay your concerns: You probably aren't gonna make it to ninety-nine.

Regardless of the ripe old age you make it to, much of your quality of life will be affected by the value others perceive you to have. And much of that perception is about the value you are able to convince others you *should* have—in other words, how well you sell yourself. And how much healthy arrogance you possess. We all assign value to things in our lives: material things, relationships, intrinsic things. Modern-day marketing is all about telling consumers how much they should care about something—a watch, a movie, a new way to meet strangers, the perfect watch to wear to the movie with the stranger you just met. And convincing others of your value isn't always about telling them how great you are. Sometimes it's about showing them how worthy you are of their support, belief, valuation.

In high school I was the chief custodial engineer at my parents' daycare center. They called me a janitor, but that's just because they didn't have a true appreciation for the scope of my talents. See how I was selling myself? Basically my parents gave me a menial job so I could learn some responsibility and they could justify paying me an allowance. No matter the title, I was the worst janitor ever. Not because I wouldn't sweep the floors, but because I never prioritized it. I always had something else to do. Like secretly practicing for the big St. Pete High School lip-synch competition, Gold Fever.

Gold Fever was *the* event at St. Pete High. People took it way too serious, and because it wasn't really a true "talent" show per se tons of people entered. I mean anybody can lip-synch, right? *But,* because of that fact, kids would go overboard with dance routines, props, even high school–level pyrotechnics. Now, to be clear, this *was not* my lane. Even though I was a popular kid, when people heard I entered the competition, they were perplexed.

"William's doing what? He's on the football team, he's the student body president, he gives speeches! But he doesn't dance. Does he?!"

I'm honestly not sure what made me go out for Gold Fever that first year. I think it was that itch of "I probably won't win . . . but what *if* I did win?" Many of my most rewarding (and questionable) decisions in life have revolved around the concept of hypothetical success. "So you're saying there's a chance?" is definitely my mentality.

I knew going into it that the odds were stacked against me. There were real dancers and performers who entered this thing. I was neither. So I immediately focused on two things. One was busting my ass and the asses of my lip-synch crew. We practiced *every* day, and since I held the esteemed position of, say it with me, *chief custodial engineer* at my parents' daycare, I had the keys and we could practice there after hours. I told my parents it would be okay that we were scuffing the floors with all the dancing we were doing at night because I would make sure they got cleaned. *{Narrator: He did not.}* I told you I was the worst.

The second thing I did was go to work selling my team. Even though there were official judges determining the winners, I knew that like in most competitions crowd participation always weighed heavily.

Time to sell. I used the fact that I was a known entity (albeit not for performing) to get an audience with as many people as I could and, like a congressional politician trying to get a bill passed, I would have intimate one-on-one conversations and confide, "Hey, listen, you know Gold Fever's coming up, right? I'm very nervous. I don't know how I'm going to do. We're working really hard and I think our show is gonna be good, *but* I'm afraid nobody is going to cheer for me. I really need you and your friends to cheer really loudly for us. You gotta have my back. Can I count on you?"

"William, of course I'm going to cheer for you," they'd say. "You're going to be okay. You're going to be fine. You can do this. Can't wait to see what you do!" I did that to fifty different people.

Because I did that meticulous "campaign" legwork, when it was showtime each of those groups felt an investment in my success. They became *part* of my team. When I came out on that stage, you would've thought I was Michael Jackson. The crowd was thunderous for me. That gave me extra confidence. I went up there and danced my little heart out to Bobby Brown's "Every Little Step." I wasn't the best dancer, my Roger Rabbit (aka the backward running man) was mediocre at best, and I didn't have the Gumby haircut Bobby had (but my black leather jacket *was* opened down to my navel). In spite of this, I *still* won first place. Why? Because I marketed myself in a way that was relevant to that audience.

I don't care if you're trying to get a date with the special someone of your dreams, a promotion at your job, or a major movie studio to buy your script, you're always going to be pitching yourself. Pitching is selling. After college, the movie thing was not happening for me right away. In college I was that guy. Everyone knew me. It was cool to be Will Packer. I was Student Supreme Court chief justice and a top radio DJ. I had made *Chocolate City,* graduated magna cum laude, then moved to Atlanta, hoping to break into the robust music video scene. I came to Atlanta with all that college swag and energy, and when I got to the ATL it was like somebody engaged the parking brake on my car. All my momentum screeched to a halt. I couldn't get my foot in the door. Nobody knew me or cared. While my peers made low six figures, I was making low six dollars per hour. All of a sudden, it wasn't so cool to be Will Packer.

I didn't want to get caught up with the responsibility and rigidity of corporate America, so, as I've mentioned, to pay the bills I got a job selling and delivering *The Atlanta Journal-Constitution* door-to-door. I did *not* want to be a salesman. I had an engineering degree for goodness' sake. A salesman sounded like somebody who travels state to state with a briefcase selling copy machines to people who don't need copy machines.

But as my dad said, "Everything is sales, son. The president of the United States is constantly selling his agenda. You want to make movies? You have to sell the movie to the people who you want to give you financing, then you've got to sell it to the people you want to go see it." He was right. It took about two days of getting doors slammed in my face and people telling me if I came back again they'd call the police for me to get the vibe and change my strategy. I had to dress a certain way, disarm people, and compliment them right off the bat. I realized I needed an opening for the 2.5 seconds I would have when the person opened the door that would allow me an "in." I'd quickly remark how lovely their landscaping looked ("Somebody worked hard on that, huh?") or act impressed with their prized muscle car parked in the driveway ("Somebody worked hard on that, huh?"). Whatever it took to connect. Then it was time for my sales pitch.

I might casually remark that the neighbor across the street had already snapped up the last of the amazing deal I was offering, and I wasn't technically supposed to sell any more, but I thought I'd take a chance with this house to see if they would want to hear it. When I put it that way, the previously angry person on the other side of the door just *had* to at least hear it. I had pushed all the buttons: I played into the scarcity factor and the greener grass factor. Before there was FOMO, there was keeping up with the Joneses.

I was selling newspapers, for sure, but I was also selling myself. I was convincing them that I was someone they could trust. Someone who was worth minutes of their time. Someone with enough healthy arrogance to convince them I had something they needed. You always have to do some version of that, and most importantly you also have to believe it yourself. And I mean *really* believe it. You have to believe in the *you* that you are selling so clearly and so passionately that the other person goes, "Okay, I believe it because you believe it." Ultimately, selling yourself is just getting other people to believe what you believe. And there's power in that. That's leadership. Leaders are able to get other people to buy into their vision. But it starts with number one, believing in your own vision. Because if you don't believe in it first, you can't do anything for anybody. You cannot be an effective leader.

The point is, it's all sales. I'm still selling myself today. Whether I'm seeking financing for my projects or trying to get people to watch or buy them. With my movies, with my TV shows, with this book, I'm constantly selling. And so are you. You're selling anything that you're doing in your life that requires somebody else's support and belief in you. It doesn't stop there. You have to sell to yourself how great you are. Remember, you're the person whose opinion matters the most. Be your harshest critic and number-one fan. Have an honest conversation with yourself, focusing on all the good you have going for you. Once you sell yourself to yourself, then you can go out and sell to the world.

LEAN IN TO WHAT YOU'RE GOOD AT

I was having a conversation with my daughter Nija the other day. I told her how in my generation, we took an aptitude test and if you scored high in math you became an engineer or mathematician. If you were good at science, you became a doctor or pharmacist. Good at public speaking? A lawyer, and so on. That was it. Widely accepted metrics told you what you should do with your life. And that's what you did. Whatever was in that bucket, that's the pigeonhole that you were thrust into.

My kids' generation has been told, "You can do anything you want. Chase your dreams! Don't settle until you find your passion!" It sounds good but that's not always helpful, and it's paralyzed them in a way. A lot of modern kids, mine included, feel like, well, I'm wasting my time doing anything until I find my true passion. Until I literally sit and find the one thing that I was put on this earth to do, everything else is meaningless. And there also are a lot of people reading this book that may be my age or older that will say, "I just don't know my dream. I don't know my passion." Stop. You sound like an after-school special. That's not how real life works. I'm not trying to kill your dreams. I'm just telling you, you can't stop doing everything until you find your dream. Don't buy into the mentality of "I'm not totally in love with something, so I'm not going to do it."

A lot of people are unhappy because they can't find the one thing that makes rainbows shoot out of their butts every morning.

Too many people feel they've failed if they haven't found their ultimate passion. The singular thing that speaks to them like no other. The thing that you just know when you see it because it's so clear and so definitive.

No, you're chasing the impossible. Stop that. You're chasing an ideal, not a practical goal.

The vast majority of people aren't doing the one singular thing that they would define as their life's passion, but that doesn't mean they can't be happy or successful or have a meaningful life. When I was selling newspapers, I whined to my dad that I didn't want to be in sales because I'm not a salesman. He said, "But that's exactly what you're good at."

By the way, Nija reminded me I wasn't always the greatest at allowing my own kids to lean in to what *they* were good at. Remember how my daughter Maya *refused* to even try to play soccer at five? Well, I had another shot at girls' soccer greatness with her older sister, Nija. In middle school Nija played on the girls' soccer team, and I was a super loud and proud soccer dad. I don't think I pushed her to play per se, but she definitely knew Dad loved the fact that she was on the team. *[Narrator: He pushed her to play.]*

Nija's challenge wasn't effort; it was more God-given ability, or lack thereof. She just wasn't a natural athlete. It didn't help that there was another girl named Alyssa on the team who was extremely talented and had a boisterous soccer dad who actually was even more loud and proud than me. *[Narrator: They were both obnoxious.]* Every game he and I would go toe-to-toe from the stands as he would cheer on his young Mia Hamm after big plays: "LEEETTT'SSS GOOOOO, ALLLYYSSSAAA!" Not to be outdone, I would cheer on my Nija just for running out on the field: "THAT'S HOW YOU DO IT, NIJA!"

One game, as I stood at the top of the bleachers plotting ways to be louder than Alyssa's dad (*Is there an actual rule against bringing cowbells to the games?),* a ball came flying right at Nija's head. She didn't have time to react. It struck her in the face at full speed. Her glasses flew straight up in the air, the ball went sideways, and she went down like a rock. I have no idea what happened in the next few moments. I must've blacked out. All I know is that I blinked and all of a sudden it was deathly silent and I was no longer at the top of the bleachers; I was standing in the middle of the field kneeling down with Nija, and everybody else was looking at me. I don't know if I flew, jumped, or teleported. All are possible by the way everyone was staring at me.

"Are you okay, baby? Are you hurt?!" I asked frantically.

"I'm fine, Daddy. Can I stop playing soccer now?"

I gave her a rousing pep talk that inspired her to dust herself off and get back out there. She became an elite middle school soccer star and even surpassed Alyssa as the best player on the team! *[Narrator: None of that last part is true. To her credit, Nija did finish the season but she never stepped foot on a soccer field afterward. Today she doesn't even like to watch soccer on TV.]*

I personally didn't grow up saying, "All I want to be is a filmmaker! All I want to be is a storyteller!" I was good at getting people together to work on projects and convincing people to go see my movies and raising money and hiring actors. I honed those skills and then I fell in love with the art of storytelling. I found a skill set that I was good at and then I found love *within* it. You've heard, "Find what you love and you'll never work a day in your life!" I'm not saying that. I'm saying, "Use your talents and what you're good at to *create* your dream life rather than waiting for it to come to you."

Be great at tangible things and find joy within those things. And if that makes rainbows shoot out of your butt, well then, you should probably get that checked.

19

Baby, You're Winning at Life

Appreciate Your Abundant Blessings

Okay, so I'm in this *very* serious fantasy football league. It's been around for more than twenty years and is comprised of a tight-knit group of super-competitive dudes. Actually, that's not totally true. One year another player's girlfriend joined, but it got uncomfortable because they broke up midseason and she continued to coach her team and proceeded to beat the snot out of not only her ex but also all the other guys in the league. The following year her ex demanded that she be ousted from the league because it was too "awkward" to have her in it. The vast majority of the other coaches agreed because it's scientifically proven that men are confident, secure creatures. We were supposed to have a vote on it, but she left voluntarily and took her coaching prowess elsewhere. Thank God.

The ex-girlfriend's one year of prominence notwithstanding, I am without a doubt the absolute best coach in our fantasy football league. This is indisputable. And whatever you do, don't ask any of the other coaches in the league because they are just a bunch of jealous haters. They would probably point out how in the two-plus decades our league has been around, I am the only owner who's been in since day one who has never won a championship. Never. Ever. Are you snickering at me, reader? I think you are. I know the sound of a snicker. You and I are the only two here, and I know *I'm* not snickering. I'm not because I know that *it's not my fault*! *{Narrator: Even I'm snickering at this point.}*

I have had the worst luck in the history of fantasy football. No matter how hard I try, no matter how much I make the right decisions and exhibit my shrewd coaching prowess, something extremely unfortunate that is out of my control *always happens.* I've had players get injured, players get suspended, and whole teams underperform, and it always happens at the worst times. One particular year I was on vacation in Mexico with Heather and my team had made it to the championship game. I vividly remember sitting on a beach in Puerto Vallarta checking the fantasy scores on my phone.

"This is the year, babe! I can feel it!" I exclaimed.

"You got this, boo!" she said as she sipped yet another margarita. She's such a great cheerleader, especially when she's tipsy. And then, like it always does, *it* happened. Something went wrong. This time my star player fumbled in the fourth quarter of the last game of the day, costing me two points. And I lost by one point.

"Nooooooo!" I yelled right there on that beach as loud as I could. Heads turned and people looked concerned . . . well, for like two seconds, then they went back to their own margaritas.

Another year down the drain. Another year of failure. Another year of not winning the chip. I sat there on a white sandy beach, with blue water and clear skies, and I just sulked. The vacation was ruined. My amazing wife chose her next words very carefully.

"Baby," she said gently, "you are winning at life."

"What?"

"You might have lost in fantasy football, but you are winning *at life.*"

She then proceeded to point out all the non-fantasy-football successes I had had that year, that week, even that day. She pointed out the abundant blessings I had received in various areas. She talked about major things, like my health, my loved ones, my career achievements. She talked about little things, like getting a great deal on the resort we were at and how it was supposed to rain that day but it hadn't.

She could have said, "Are you serious? You're getting upset about a stupid game? Get over yourself and look at the view in front of you. You are tripping!" But my wife knows me. She knows how passionate and competitive I am. She knows that the drive and energy that I pour into my fake football team is pulled from the same well of passion that has propelled my real movie career. She's careful not to diminish or minimize my passion. She just encourages me to shift my perspective toward the positive. She doesn't judge what's important to me in that moment, but she reminds me of the importance of a balanced life and the fact that I'm winning more than I'm losing.

She does that periodically. When I get upset about and consumed by some small failing or defeat, she'll simply say, "Baby, winning at life." And it undoubtedly settles me down.

That way of thinking has helped me to appreciate my victories in a broader sense.

It's helped me to understand that setbacks and disappointments in one area don't define my worth or overshadow my achievements in others. I'm now better able to recognize the danger of allowing a single event to diminish my self-confidence and happiness. No matter what that event might be.

I'm like a lot of type-A personalities who latch on to challenges of varying significance to help fuel my competitive spirit. Michael Jordan and his legendary fictional rivalries come to mind. I know I have a need to channel my drive in productive ways. But I also realize the importance of keeping perspective and not letting it derail my self-worth or contentment.

When disappointments arise, we have to remind ourselves of the invaluable blessings that surround us. We have to understand that true success lies not in a single victory but in living a fulfilled and meaningful existence.

Generally, I'm a macro-perspective guy, but I, like everybody else, do get caught up in the minutiae sometimes: I wore the wrong shoes, I'm behind on my to-do list, my fantasy football tight end is enchanted with Taylor Swift and can't shake it off. But I try to keep my view and self-judgment at a thirty-thousand-foot perspective.

We all spend too much time attaching our worth to what's immediately in front of our faces, whether it matters in the greater scheme of things or not. We can't do that; our worth is too valuable, much more valuable than the trivial stuff. When you feel yourself getting caught up in the small stuff, step back and look at the broader picture.

Sometimes very driven people feel like they have to win at everything. A loss of any kind is still a loss, and we don't like to lose. That's how we are. It's a characteristic of being so competitive. If you are one of those people too, it's fine. Whether you're the CEO of a multinational corporation or just launching your start-up, be passionate and give 110 percent, but not at the expense of you feeling like you're not winning at life, because you are.

After Heather said those sage words to me in Mexico, I turned to her and said, "That was such an incredible way to put that, baby. I love you so much."

"And another one!" she said.

"Exactly. Next year I'll win the championship and then another one!"

She turned drunkenly from the waiter she had just finished ordering with and said, "What championship?"

20

Please Stop Helping Me

Always Set Your Own Bar

Those who genuinely want the best for us don't always tell us what's best for us. Put another way: The people who love us often don't realize they're the ones holding us back. They (usually) don't do it out of malice or envy; it's often about them trying to protect us. They want to shield us from the negativity and disappointment of the big bad world, and they think if they roll us up in metaphorical bubble wrap, then maybe we won't get hurt or have to deal with failure or heartbreak. Know anybody like that in your life?

I ran track in middle school. Now, the track team wasn't racially segregated per se. But there were *no* white guys that ran short-distance events and no Black dudes who ran cross-country long distance. We always did a mile-long warm-up run as a team before every practice. The cross-country kids left us sprinters in the dust because we just weren't used to that pace for that distance. One day, a white kid named Craig got to practice late and had to play catch-up during the warm-up mile. As he booked past me, I instinctively ran faster, fell into his rhythm, and kept up with him. Before I knew it, I was running the fastest that I had ever run for more than a few hundred yards, and I was thinking, "I'm really doing this. I need to ask my mom if we have Kenyan roots."

That's when one of my closest track homies yelled out, "What are you doing, Packer? We don't run like that! Are you crazy? You're gonna tire yourself out!"

The long-distance boys were always trying to break their personal records in the mile. Nobody expected *us* to really *run* a mile. We always jogged it. That was the point. That's all we had to do. I was like, "You know what? You're right. What am I doing? That's not me. That's not what I do."

I was keeping up with this kid; I was right there with him. But I immediately slowed down and fell back in with my crew and continued to have the mediocre track career that I lie to my kids about to this day. It's not that my track mates were hating on me. They were just saying, "Hey, Will, relax. You don't need to do all that; protect yourself."

Some part of me has always wondered, "What if I had kept going and beat Craig? Did I have untapped potential as a runner that I never explored?" It's a question that lingers in my mind. I guess I'll never know. I'll never know what my limits were because I didn't push myself. Did I miss an opportunity to be the next Haile Gebrselassie? "Who?" you ask. He's the GOAT of long-distance running. Duh. *{Narrator: Will had to Google his name and how to pronounce it.}*

I get it. You're thinking, "That's a middle school track story, Will. I'm about to leave my corporate job and try entrepreneurship, or take a leap and transition into another field, or graduate from college and foray into a completely different area." Yep, I hear you. And I can relate. The summer before my senior year of college, I called my parents to tell them I was forgoing my final engineering internship at Motorola so I could stay in Tallahassee and work on our fledgling production company. It wasn't a conversation I wanted to have. In fact, the whole "What are you doing after you graduate?" line of questioning that college kids hate usually reaches a fever pitch right before graduation. I was stirring up that hornet's nest a whole year in advance. The reason was Rob Hardy and I felt that if we were going to be serious about chasing our dream of becoming filmmakers, we needed to start putting the time in right then. We needed to be as prepared as possible to take the full entrepreneurial leap when we graduated a year later. This was especially tricky for me because I had been a stellar intern at Motorola for the previous two years. Skipping the final all-important junior-year internship meant that I was basically passing up an all-but-guaranteed job offer.

None of this was lost on my parents. I knew what I was up against, so I had my pitch ready. I assured them that I was still going to complete my electrical engineering degree like I had promised. I reminded them how when I agreed to accept a scholarship in a field I wasn't passionate about, they told me after graduation I could pursue my entrepreneurial endeavors. I told them that this was the time to chase this dream, not later once I got in the corporate rat race. It would be much harder to take this leap once I had a corporate paycheck, mortgage, car note, and so on. I was passionate but logical. I had thought this through. I felt I was pretty convincing. I waited for the parents who'd raised me to chase my dreams and shoot for the stars to respond.

"This makes no sense, William," my mom lamented. "Why would you pass up on the stability of a job at a major corporation? Do you know how hard it is to feed yourself out in the real world? Have you *really* thought this through?" And just like that my mom touched on every single one of my main anxiety areas. But I was steadfast in my conviction, and I pushed back on all her cons with my own pros. But the reality is that it was unnerving not to have the full support and enthusiasm of someone so important in my life.

My dad took a much more dispassionate approach, telling my mom, "If that is what he wants to do, then we have to let him. He won't let himself starve." Ummm, thanks, Dad, I think.

I'm awfully glad I took the leap of faith and that I did it when I did. My mom had been an ardent supporter from day one. She had done everything she could to ensure my success all the way up to that point. She wanted what she thought was best for me. She didn't want me to struggle. She didn't want me to fail. She was afraid I was choosing a life path that made both more likely.

People who love you can project their own fears onto you. But you must never ever let someone else dampen your potential by projecting their own risk tolerance onto you. You have to set your own bar—how high you want to (and ultimately do) soar is up to you and you alone. Never forget that. You don't owe outside people, even those who want the best for you, anything but to listen and hear them out. But you owe it to yourself to test your limits and take whatever risks you have to, to excel.

There's a balance between considering the caution and care of those around us and taking risks to chase our dreams. It's about knowing when to listen and when to trust our own instincts. We can't let the fear of failure or the opinions of others hold us back from exploring new possibilities. This is also healthy arrogance.

There's nothing wrong with having people around who want to give well-meaning advice. They're valuable. They're in your corner. They're your support system. However, don't overvalue the opinions of anybody who's not you. Just like my mom said all the things I was already subconsciously fearful of, your inner circle knows you well. That means they know your strengths, your weaknesses, and your biggest areas of concern. That can make their advice sound pretty foolproof. But you might surprise even yourself with the choices you make and the risks you take when you *allow* yourself the license to make the best decisions for you. Follow your instincts, your drive, your dream. You get the final say. Liken it to being the chairman and CEO of your own company and having a board of directors. Listen carefully to everybody's thoughts and opinions, but, ultimately, it's your final decision. Don't relinquish that power.

Funny enough, as I'm writing this, I've actually started running long distances. By the time you read this, I may have even won a marathon. And by *won* I mean run and by *run* I mean completed in some form or fashion. Doesn't matter. I'm going to push myself and nobody can stop me this time. Or you. Take that, middle school track homies. Look at me now.

21

All You Need Is One (White) Guy

Advocacy Is a Two-Way Street

"Here's what I tell Black coaches and, unfortunately, it's just part of the deal: 'All you need is one. One white guy in your corner who has the power of leverage.'" This is a quote from NFL coordinator Harold Goodwin about Super Bowl–winning coach Bruce Arians. Goodwin uses this quote regarding race because in the NFL there is an extreme disparity between the number of Black players and the number of Black coaches. Arians (a white head coach) put his convictions front and center when he won the Super Bowl in 2021 as the only team with Black coordinators for his offense, defense, and special teams. Hollywood, on the other hand, is one of the most progressive, liberal industries, and it's *still* pretty much a white patriarchal frat house, one of the whitest clubs in the world. Mostly white men and a few white women at the highest levels. We have a long way to go.

Being Black in Hollywood and dealing with a power structure that primarily rewards and advances white executives is definitely a challenge, but my advice here applies to any industry where there are not a lot of minorities with power . . . which, by the way, is every industry. Having said that, this is not just about race. It's not just about the color of your skin; it's about power and access—who has it and who is willing to help equitably distribute it. In that sense your "one white guy" may not be white or a guy.

To stick with this analogy, if you need just one white guy, make sure it's the right white guy. Sometimes all you need is one advocate, the right type of person who believes passionately in your vision. Nobody does anything by themselves. I don't care who you are or how talented you are. Everybody needs someone in a position of power in their corner. If you want to be on the path to greatness, you must align yourself with the right people who can help unlock something for you that you would otherwise not have access to or be able to attain.

My one white guy was Clint Culpepper. When I was an up-and-coming filmmaker hustling my way into Hollywood, Clint ran Screen Gems, the genre division of Sony Studios. I met Clint because after *Trois* came out and made some money independently, it was his office that called me about it when I was at home in my boxer shorts and pretending to be my own assistant.

Afterward we made *The Gospel* for the home video division of Sony. Clint saw it, loved it, and realized it could do more than just DVD numbers, and he gave the green light to release it theatrically. Clint actually pissed off people at Sony because he gave us money and a marketing budget to go out and promote the film on our own, in the same way that we had promoted *Trois* and *Chocolate City* independently. Clint's philosophy was, "Hey, these guys have been doing it without our big, expensive, slow, clunky system. Let's give them some more resources and see what they can do their way." He authorized it himself.

Later, some higher-ups found out and complained, "What the hell are you doing? We don't just give filmmakers money to go out and buy flyers and do promotions at churches and conventions. That's not how this works, Clint."

Clint was like, "Well, we do now." Only he could say that. He took a risk and bucked the system. That's the white guy you want in your corner.

More important, I didn't let Clint down. We made *The Gospel* for $3 million and it made $15 million, five times the budget. He gave me that opportunity, and I proved myself worthy. I delivered. That's very, very important. We made Clint look smart for taking a chance on us. Make someone advocating for you look good and they'll never stop championing you.

That was the beginning of a very fruitful friendship/business relationship. Clint was looking for projects that could appeal to an African American audience, and I had tons of ideas I just needed the resources to make. I knew the types of projects Clint wanted to make. His affinity for African American audiences and my story-telling ability and knowledge of these audiences proved to be a very potent combo. I knew he needed me to deliver box office with these projects so his bosses would allow him to continue funding them. And deliver I did. I delivered over and over again. I said I was going to do something, and then I did it. I harken back to what my Hudlin brother sensei told me when I was just a doe-eyed young go-getter: "Always be a doer, not a talker."

If you look at my early filmography—*Obsessed, Takers, No Good Deed, Stomp the Yard, Think Like a Man,* and *Think Like a Man Too*—that was all Clint and me. And they all opened at the top. That's six number ones I made with him.

I remember the first time I met Clint, thinking, "How is this person in a position of power?" He was such a unicorn. In Hollywood, the land of interesting characters, he remains one of the most interesting. He is loud, gay, brash, and just loves him some Black folks and Black culture. He would sometimes say that he felt like a

Black woman trapped in a white man's body. "Let's just keep that between us, Clint," I would respond. Suffice to say, he was passionate. Surprisingly, we had a lot in common. We were both from Florida, we were both outsiders, and we both went against the grain. Neither of us were in the position we were in because we did things in a traditional way. He wasn't like any exec that you'd ever meet. He would rather be out doing shots of tequila with the actors than sitting at some desk poring over cost reports.

Clint's a little cray, but he was my guy. {Narrator: Will's a little cray too. That's why it worked.} Looking at us side by side, we didn't make sense. But you can never count people out or judge books by their covers. Your guy or gal may not be somebody who looks like someone you grew up with or know a lot about. Your guy or gal may be somebody completely out of your sphere. My champion happened to be a white gay dude from Pensacola, Florida.

I've had strong relationships with a few executives in my career. The key to those relationships is always figuring out what's important to them. It could be social messaging, huge box-office numbers, or the simple gesture of picking up the check at the Polo Club in Beverly Hills. I broke into an exclusive, closed club and learned to navigate it because I figured out what was important to those executives. What were their hot buttons? Did they want to win awards? Just make boatloads of money? Win a weekend? With *Stomp the Yard*, they didn't want to make the movie I wanted to make, but I positioned it into the movie that they thought they wanted to make. And then I got to tell my story. Remember that advocacy is a two-way street. You need someone to be an ally for you, but you need to reciprocate by making them feel like backing you was the right decision. In order to deliver for them, you have to be very attentive to learn what they value. This skill can be advantageous across multiple aspects of your life.

One of my favorite books is Dale Carnegie's *How to Win Friends and Influence People*. One of the things he talks about is the power of being a good conversationalist. I always tell my kids when they've got a big interview or meeting, "Okay, put the Carnegie on 'em." Which means, get the other person to talk about themselves because that's most people's favorite subject and what they're most comfortable talking about. And through them talking about them, you find places to insert yourself. At the end of it, the person inevitably thinks, "I really like that Will Packer!" even though they talked about themselves for 60 percent of the interview!

One approach I use in conversation is when people ask about me, I turn it on them and ask them to tell me their life story. When they ask where I'm from, I'll say, "I'm from St. Pete, Florida, beautiful city, amazing beaches. Where are you from? You're from New York? Really? I just left there. What do you love about the city? What's your favorite part?" Now we've already shifted. We're talking about you.

There is a lot of conversation in traditional business settings around code-switching. For people of color it's been a matter of survival in many spaces. But can you still be your authentic self while adjusting your language and syntax to assimilate to "majority" culture? The answer is yes . . . to a degree. No matter your ethnicity or background, when you're just starting off in a new environment it matters what the decision makers, no matter what they look like or where they're from, think of you. You will be judged on how comfortable they feel doing business with you. But that doesn't mean you need to abandon who you truly are in order to succeed. It means you may have to put the work in to get others to see the unique value you bring *because* of your different culture and perspective. What that looks like and *sounds* like is up to you given the situation. But ultimately the burden is on you to be a valuable element to someone who can in turn be essential to your growth and development. If you do that and they still don't see you as vital and worth advocating for, then that's their loss. They were never the right voice to have on your side anyway.

Harold Goodwin was right—a single well-positioned supporter can make all the difference. Put in work to find them, bring value to the relationship, and be open to unexpected allies. Your one person might be a Keisha trapped in the body of a Clint; doesn't matter. That right someone with power on your side is an essential step on the path to success.

22

If All Else Fails, Open a Fruit Stand

The Benefits of Fearlessness

I always remind myself not to take everything so seriously. I'm not saving lives, I'm just entertaining them. I've learned to protect my joy, but I wasn't always like that. It took almost being exiled in a foreign country to really embrace living my life this way.

Around Christmastime in 2009, I had just wrapped a sequel to *Stomp the Yard* called *Stomp the Yard: Homecoming,* and I decided to take a new lady friend I was dating on vacation to Jamaica. I'd met this lovely lady earlier that year on a riverboat cruise in New Orleans during the Essence Festival of Culture. I had gone to the riverboat with Idris Elba, who was "hosting" the party on board, which really meant he had to show up at the beginning, take a few pictures with fans, then sneak off the boat before it ever left the dock. She was there because she was working for the brand that sponsored the event. Her job was to show up, make sure the various branded promotions and activations were being executed properly, then also leave before the boat sailed.

But a funny thing happened. When it was time for Idris and our crew to leave, I couldn't find some of the folks I brought with us. Idris said, "You can stay and find your friends, but I gotta get off this boat now; otherwise, I'll be stuck for two hours while it sails the Mississippi River and I can't do that because I have three other parties to host." Before I could ask him how many parties he was hosting at the same time, he bolted.

On the other side of the boat, the lovely lady tasked with overseeing the brands was having a hard time wrangling her crew as well. By the time she gathered her girlfriends and was heading toward the exit, they realized the boat was pulling away from the dock. And that's how we both ended up stuck on a boat we had tried to get off of.

I was smitten the first time I set eyes on her. She could not have cared less the first time she saw me. I was just another dude on a boat that it was clear she didn't want to be on. I needed an ice-breaker of some sort. Being the persistent Packer that I am, I had my friend, who was very drunk I should mention, go over to the table and attempt to talk to her and her crew. When that went predictably horrendously, I showed up just in the nick of time ostensibly to apologize for him and make sure the ladies were good and didn't need anything. I introduced myself to each person at the table, and when I got to the hazel-eyed beauty I had my eye on the whole time, I said, "My name is Will, and you are?"

"Heather," she replied.

Cut to five months later and the two of us are standing in line at Hartsfield-Jackson Atlanta International Airport about to take our first major trip together. I like to think when Heather met me, she figured since I was a fancy movie producer, I must be very responsible and put-together. I was certainly trying to project that image when we were checking in and the woman at the counter looked at my passport and asked, "Do you have another one?"

I laughed. "I know, the picture's not great, but I look like Usher Raymond on my driver's license photo."

Heather giggled. The woman did not.

"Your passport is expired," she said with a straight face.

The good thing with passports is you have ten years to renew them. The bad thing is you have ten years to renew them. So that means you never think about it! I did not think about it. I was like, "Are you [bleeping] kidding me?" Not a good look in front of my new boo. Now she thinks I'm the type of person who doesn't handle their responsibilities. And I'm actually the opposite. I actually do handle my responsibilities. But you couldn't tell on this particular day.

Being that the flight was in two hours, there was no way I could rectify this in time. Based on it being a Friday and us needing to be back the following Tuesday, pushing the trip didn't really make sense either. "Do you want to cancel the trip?" Heather asked.

Now, while Heather's energy told me that she would have gone with the flow and if we had to cancel the trip, she would've been disappointed but not made a big deal out of it, all I heard when she asked me that was, *"So we gotta cancel this trip because I'm with the guy who doesn't pay attention to important things like passport renewals and I should have never given you my number on that boat and I should have left when Idris Elba left but instead I'm at the airport about to go to another country with a guy that can't complete simple tasks, huh?"*

"Don't worry," I said to Heather. "You go ahead through security and I'll meet you at the gate."

"Wait, what are you going to do?" she asked.

I replied, "Don't question me, woman. Don't you know you're with the type of man who handles things, and even when things don't go according to plan I figure the shit out? I may not be Idris Elba, but I'm a big boss movie producer, damn it!" *{Narrator: That's actually not what Will said at all.}*

"Don't worry about me, babe. I'll see you at the gate."

She left, and I went into figure-this-out-by-any-means-necessary mode like my life depended on it. My desire to impress my new woman aside, I really couldn't imagine canceling this trip. You know how it is when you have a cool trip planned. You look forward to it for weeks. You've tried on your outfits. The date can't come fast enough. I wasn't sure if I could actually figure this out, but I was gonna go down fighting. First I had to get a gate pass to get past security. I'd been flying back and forth from Atlanta to L.A. so much that I had gotten to know several of the employees. And I'm the type of person who always tries to speak and be cordial to everyone. Especially to workers in support staff roles. It's the right thing to do, and you never know when you might need them.

I was able to get somebody at the airline I had met in my travels to get me a gate pass that you use to pick up your kids if they're flying unaccompanied. That got me past TSA, which was step number one. Now I had to figure out how to physically get on the plane. My analytical brain was saying, "One step at a time." One of my favorite quotes is from the TV series *House of Cards,* when a character plotting a massive power grab says, "How do you swallow a whale? One bite at a time." Time for the next bite.

Generally speaking, airline employees who work at the gates can be a mean and surly bunch. I can't blame them. All day they're having to deal with crying babies, panicked people running late, and dudes trying to sneak onto international flights with expired passports. At the gate for our Jamaica flight, there was a particularly irritable woman who looked like she *really* didn't want to be there. "Have your boarding pass and passports out!" Grumpy Gertrude yelled as the flight began boarding. I was standing with Heather, realizing I was probably the only person trying to get on the flight who didn't have a valid version of either.

As other passengers started to crowd the boarding area, I told Heather to hang back until I could determine if I could get on. I genuinely wasn't sure if I could, and I didn't want her to board without me, fly to Jamaica by herself, and end up smoking weed and listening to Bob Marley on the beach with some muscly dreadlocked Rasta.

I bided my time as the boarding area got more and more packed. One thing about airline people, they're trying to get the flights out on time because they get graded on that. I waited until there was a massive crush at the gate and the boarding doors were near closing. I intentionally went right up to Grumpy Gertrude.

"Where's your boarding pass?!"

"I'm so sorry. I think I dropped it."

"Uggghhh!" she sighed with all the undertones of "You are *so* pissing me off right now." She rolled her eyes. "This means I gotta print you another pass."

She was so focused on trying to quickly print me a boarding pass she only checked the name on my passport, not the expiration. This was before *everything* was digital, mind you. "Here!" she said gruffly, shoving the boarding pass at me.

"You're amazing!" I replied and winked at Heather.

We get to our seats on the plane and I'm grinning ear to ear, visions of Red Stripe and rum punch circling in my head.

Not so fast. For some reason after everyone was boarded the plane wasn't leaving the gate. It was just sitting there, delayed, for twenty minutes past departure time, and the flight crew wasn't giving us any updates. I hate it when they do that. Today it was giving me a panic attack. I was coming unglued, thinking they looked at the manifest and discovered that my passport wasn't right. At some point Grumpy Gertrude herself came on the plane and started walking down the aisle toward our seats. Everything moved in slow motion as I realized I was about to get dragged off this plane in front of Heather and everybody else. I was drenched in sweat as she walked right past me without even a glance. They were looking for someone else. It wasn't until the plane actually took off that I realized my sphincter had been clenched tight for thirty minutes. Once in the air I screamed "Wooooooo!" like a tenth-grade girl who just made the cheerleading team.

"You're crazy!" Heather said.

"Crazy for you," I said cheesily as I put my arm around her.

A few hours later we landed in Jamaica, and the next challenge was clearing customs. I think I was hoping that once I landed they might not even check passports because you're already in the country. But you know how when you're thinking of buying a particular car, all of a sudden everywhere you look you start seeing that type of car? Before that trip I had never noticed how many signs there were when you arrive in a foreign country reading, "Have your passport out."

"Must have passport."

"Will Packer, we're talking to you."

These signs were everywhere. So now I'm thinking, "What have I done? I flew all the way over here without a valid passport. What if they won't let me in? Do they fly me back to America? Do I have to sit in some grimy detention center with Jamaican murderers until they sort it out?" We're in line for customs and my brain is going a million miles a minute. There were two customs lines: One had an older woman checking credentials and the other had a young guy working the desk. When it was our turn the woman was open but I told the couple behind us they could go first. Heather looked at me curiously. When the guy's line opened, I turned to Heather. "You gotta go first. I need you to distract this guy."

"Distract him how?"

"However you can." I shrugged.

Now it was Heather's turn to wink at me.

I knew my best chance was to have a hot American chick flirting with this young Jamaican dude. And Heather didn't disappoint. She and I still laugh to this day thinking about how she was batting those big beautiful hazel eyes at him and asking him ditzy I've-never-been-to-Jamaica-can-you-tell-me-what-I-should-do questions. As she heartily laughed at his corny jokes, he looked over at me and I acted completely unfazed like her cousin or brother would. He was still busy talking to her as he manually checked my passport (don't try this in the digital era, kids) and gave me the coveted entry stamp. I was officially in Jamaica!

On the way to the resort I called Shayla Cowan, my newly hired executive assistant at the time, who technically didn't even start until a few weeks later. One of the reasons I was excited about hiring her was that she had a ton of relationships. "I know you don't start until January," I whispered out of Heather's earshot, "but I'm going to need a little help right now. I just landed in Jamaica with my girlfriend, and I have an expired passport. See what you can do."

"How in the world did you get into the country?"

"It doesn't matter. I'm here now."

"How are you gonna get back?!"

"That's why I'm calling you. You've got four days to figure it out."

Silence

I was praying she wouldn't say, "You know what, this job is probably not a good fit for me. No, thanks."

"Look," I said. "See what you can do. Maybe you can get me back, maybe not. I think I really like Heather. I think it's going in a good direction. If you can't get me back, maybe she and I can stay and open up a fruit stand."

"You are crazy!" she said.

"Not the first time I've heard that today."

"I'll call you back."

I had no real plan to get back. At that point I didn't care. I went and had an absolute blast with Heather. I didn't spend every day thinking about my predicament. Once I knew there was nothing I could do about it from there and Shayla was doing all she could in the background, I figured my job was to give 110 percent into having the best trip ever. Otherwise, what was the point of all I went through to get there?! The storyteller in me thinks it would be kinda cool if I was writing this book from Jamaica in between running a chain of fruit stands with Heather because I never got out. But alas, Shayla's Rolodex had serious depth. I won't expound too much, but the short version is Shayla called Ludacris's manager, Chaka Zulu, who knew the actor Tommy Ford (yep, Martin Lawrence's sidekick on *Martin*. RIP), who actually had been wanting to be in one of my movies and whose ex happened to work in immigration. You follow all that? Getting out did require me to leave the turquoise water of Montego Bay and drive three hours to the U.S. embassy in Kingston, but that was a small price to pay for one helluva trip.

That first trip with Heather almost didn't happen. In a purely pragmatic sense, it probably shouldn't have. But that's no way to live the greatest life possible. I don't just mean from a pure enjoyment standpoint. I mean from an accomplishment and success outlook as well. Some of the greatest decisions you'll make may not make sense on paper. You might have to start the metaphorical international flight not knowing how you're going to get back. But once you've decided to do something, give it your all no matter what. No sense in dwelling on the drawbacks at that point.

While Shayla was working furiously behind the scenes to get me home from Jamaica, I kept telling her, much to her dismay, "Don't worry. If it doesn't work out, I'll just stay here." I was joking, mostly. I wasn't going to let the possibility of failure ruin the moment. Shayla always uses this story to explain why I have the successful career I have. She says I'm fearless. That I just put my shoulders back and walk tall into whatever situation, no matter the circumstance.

I am somebody who always thinks, "What if?" The "what if" drives me, the possibility of success and how great it would be if I indeed succeed. When I'm trying to reach the top of a mountain, the fact that I could fall to my death twenty thousand feet off the side is not as important as the possibility of standing at the summit with my arms outstretched. In the angels-on-the-shoulder motif, my "cautious" angel doesn't stand a chance because my "risk" angel is so much louder. The cautious angel gets drowned out because I'm thinking if I reach the top of the mountain, I can plant a big ol' flag with a *P* on it.

Heather and I have been inseparable since that Jamaica trip. We got married. Built an incredible life together. And she's been in charge of the passports ever since.

23

Really Keep It Real. Really.

There Is a Premium Placed on Authenticity

Authenticity is so important. We're all craving truth and genuine-ness, and we're all connected now in ways that we never were before. We're interacting with people from various demographics, subcultures, and parts of the world that are unfamiliar and we may never have had access to previously. We're getting a chance to peek into people's lives, which makes all of our authenticity radars better and sharper. People can sniff out a fake much easier than they ever could before.

A director I know well once told me a very emotional story about how hard it had been for them to make it up the Hollywood ladder because another higher-profile director had basically "stolen" their position in the industry. The more famous director had risen by doing the exact same type of filmmaking the director I knew had been honing for years, but now it was known as the other director's signature style. This director described the pain of trying to come up in an industry where everyone thought they were basically copying someone who in fact had copied them first. They were so passionate, they started to cry as they were telling me this. They told me they were only speaking about this because they felt we were close and it wasn't something they would normally share. It was really powerful to have them open up to me, and I truly empathized with them.

The story stuck with me. I felt their pain and started giving serious thought to opportunities I may be able to create for us to work together. Soon after, I was speaking with a peer in the industry who was looking for a director for a project and I started to relay the story. It caught me completely off guard when this person interrupted me and finished telling *me* the person's story, word for word. Replaying the tears and all.

That moment surgically removed the heart from the story. My peer told me that this person had told that story a thousand times before. I thought this director and I had shared a private moment—I didn't know everyone in town had heard his sob story too. The crazy thing is that even though the anguish could have been absolutely genuine and valid, the repetition to multiple people made it lose all its impact. Now it just felt performative. Looking back, it felt like they were acting the whole time telling me the story. My friends, passion is good, passion is important, passion gets people's attention. *But* for the love of baby Jesus, make sure it's real and genuine passion. If you can't be truly passionate about something, don't fake it because it's worse when people find out you're an impostor. They feel like you lied to them. Now they can't trust anything about you.

Hollywood is known for its fakery—it's a cliché but, unfortunately, a well-deserved one. This industry is legendary for its superficiality, faux compliments, and empty promises. I have countless stories of agents badmouthing their own clients in an attempt to ingratiate themselves with me or get something they think will make them look good with their client.

"You know how wishy-washy Tom Cruise can be. Everybody

knows. It drives me crazy!" an agent will say. "Go ahead and make an offer to him now for the project before he gets flaky again."

I'm thinking, "I know you want the offer for your client, but there's probably a better way to frame it."

Then, in front of Tom Cruise, they're all, "OMG, I was just saying to Will how amazing you are about setting your mind to something and sticking to it," as they turn to me for confirmation. *So now you're pulling me into your fakeness?! {Narrator: The comment about Tom Cruise is totally made up. Though would it be a total surprise if somebody somewhere did actually say that about Tom Cruise? None of us are immune to the fakery, even Tom.}*

I think about authenticity a lot as a filmmaker, because I'm always trying to make things that will resonate with audiences who have an overabundance of choices.

I'll let you in on one of the secrets to my success as a filmmaker. Not only do I always think about the core audience I'm making content for, I think about them in a very specific way. I always start with a particular distinct person who is in the core audience. Then I fill out this person's fictional world. I name this person and I give them a job and kids and quirks and likes and dislikes. Now I start thinking about how I'm delivering something specifically for them. I will literally tell my creative team, "Okay, this one is for Sharonda in Detroit who's got two kids and she works at the pharmacy. She is secretly working on launching an e-retail business on the side. She hates her boss. Right now, she puts up with him because it's a stable paycheck and she needs the healthcare. She's currently single because she divorced the father of her kids three years ago when she caught him wearing her panties and flirting online with a guy who lived two streets over. He swears nothing happened, and she might have been able to get past it, but they were her good panties and he totally stretched them out. All she wants to do is come home, drink a glass of white Zinfandel every now and then, and go to the movies on Friday night. And when she goes, she doesn't have time for a movie that's depressing. She doesn't like horror. She wants to laugh, and she wants to see herself on-screen. She doesn't care if the person on-screen is imperfect because she's imperfect. She just wants an escape. And her version of an escape is being able to laugh at a world that feels familiar yet heightened to her."

And *that* was my specific *Girls Trip* audience example. Sharonda. If I have any gift, it is being able to present authentic stories to audiences with the right actors who authentically portray the characters in those stories. One of the reasons that movie was so successful was the genuineness of Tiffany Haddish, who played the wild woman Dina. *Girls Trip* was her big breakout role. Everybody else who auditioned for that role did admirable jobs of portraying the character that was on the page. And we had some big-name actors that came out. But Tiffany didn't portray that character; she disappeared into the role. It didn't feel like she was acting. She took what was on the page and brought it to life in a genuine way. Unlike that director with the sob story, she was dripping with authenticity. She took the Dina character and made it completely her own, which the best actors always do. I knew Sharonda would love her.

For *Ride Along,* my target was Cody, a young white male teenager in Miami. He went to public school, played on the soccer team, listened to hip-hop, and loved the comedy of Kevin Hart. He didn't have a girlfriend, so all he wanted to do on a Saturday night was go to the movies at the mall with his boys. Cody shows up at the mall at noon even though he hasn't finished his homework and the movie doesn't start until six-thirty. He gets dropped off by his parents, walks around all day, hopes to get a couple phone numbers from girls, eats a slice at Sbarro, and peruses the sneaker shop even though he won't buy anything because he didn't get his allowance yet. He's self-conscious about his smile, so he covers his mouth when he laughs. His mom keeps promising braces, but they're expensive and he's got three older brothers who never got them so they're hating on him getting some. Cody loves watching comedy skits on You-Tube. That was my *Ride Along* guy.

When I'm developing a script, creating such specificity around my target audience helps me so much because then I know exactly who I'm making it for. I'm like, Sharonda's gonna think this is fake. Or Cody's going to think this isn't funny enough. I lean on my Codys and Sharondas to cast my movies too. Who's cool to Cody? Who makes this a *must-see* for Sharonda?

Focusing on audience specificity extends beyond developing the movie and into the marketing. For *Ride Along* we went straight after the Codys with promotions like a viral skit with Ice Cube, Kevin Hart, and Conan O'Brien riding together in a car. Cody loves him some Conan O'Brien. During our campaign for *Girls Trip* I brought the entire cast to the Essence Festival of Culture for events, special screenings, and an appearance on the main stage in front of sixty thousand fans. The Sharondas went crazy.

I believe that in an oversaturated content environment you have to make a movie for *an* audience. Not necessarily *every* audience, but certainly a very specific one. And as a producer you need to be intentional about it. Some filmmakers want to make four-quadrant movies. That means their audience is everyone: young, old, male, female; they want everybody. I've always said if you can get a specific audience, you nail that audience and other audiences will come. I have certainly benefited from having a core audience of African Americans (especially women) who are influential to other audiences. That's led me to the top of the box-office charts over and over again. The other movies I went up against on those weekends often had what some would say were bigger stars; almost certainly they had larger production and marketing budgets. However, they didn't have what I had: a consistent, dedicated, persuasive audience who felt ownership of a project that felt authentic to them.

Whatever your industry, don't just jump in with fake passion around something you think your intended audience is passionate about. Don't say you love cats if you hate cats. You don't have to have a commonality around that specific passion, but perhaps there's a commonality around some other aspect, like leadership or humanity. If you come in and you try to fake it, people will find out. And save the tears; both Cody *and* Sharonda will know they're fake.

24

Stay in Your Lane (Just Make It Wide)

Lean in to Your Thing

I like to think everyone knows a Will Packer project when they see it. I've excelled with projects that have universal themes told through a very specific lens. Oftentimes my core audience is African American women. I've often said, "Black women have the keys to the kingdom." They always have, but nobody ever paid enough attention. I've always paid attention to them. And they've supported me throughout my career, so I make it a priority to continue to feed that audience. I do it consistently and reliably. Focusing on a specific area of your job is essential.

In my high school football days, there was a defining moment that taught me a valuable lesson about staying in your lane. I was playing cornerback, and during a practice there were some girls watching as the offense attempted a wide receiver pass. As a cornerback in a zone defense, my responsibility was to stay back and cover the deep third of the field.

The quarterback threw a lateral pass to the wide receiver in front of me, who was not my responsibility. Fueled by the excitement and the attention from the girls, I immediately ran toward him and unleashed a ferocious hit, causing the guy to fumble the ball. Cheers and applause filled the air, and I basked in the momentary glory of my play. However, Coach Wiz quickly pulled me aside. "Do you hear all those people cheering for you? Feels good, doesn't it? But let me tell you something. You were undisciplined and left your assigned area. That was a third-string player who couldn't get the second pass off in time to the receiver who was wide open in your zone. In a real game, with a skilled player on the field, he would have thrown a touchdown pass while you were out of position. And you know what those people cheering for you would say then? 'What the [bleep] is wrong with Packer?!' You messed up."

Ouch. In that moment of glory, I had lost sight of the importance of fulfilling my role within the team. While I received praise for the big hit, it ultimately didn't matter because I had neglected my responsibility. I prioritized short-term recognition over executing my job properly. I thought I had done so well, but I lost sight of what I was supposed to be doing. I got lucky I didn't get burned that time. But if I kept it up, someone was eventually going to blow past me and catch a touchdown or three. I lost track of the bigger picture. I needed to do my job.

In life, we often find ourselves juggling multiple responsibilities, chasing various goals, and navigating countless distractions. It can be easy to lose sight of what truly matters and allow our focus to scatter. But amid the noise, it is crucial to remember the powerful mantra, "Keep the main thing the main thing."

That's not to say you should never branch out and try new things. Sometimes we don't want to be defined by a single project or association. In the beginning of my career, I was known as one of the "guys that made *Chocolate City*," and of course that made me proud. However, as time went on, I grew tired of being boxed into that label. Then came *Trois,* and suddenly I was the "*Trois* guy" and yearning to break out of that box. Everywhere I would go in my world, when people introduced me, they'd say, "Hey, this is the guy that made *Trois*." *{Narrator: And most times they'd still pronounce it wrong.}* They pigeonholed me, and I had to fight to get out of it. I wanted to be known as more than just the guy who made one specific movie.

I yearned to break out of that box, but the cycle continued with each new project. I was defined in the eyes of others. I worked with incredible individuals like Sony exec Clint Culpepper and Kevin Hart, and their contributions were valuable, but I had to prove that my success wasn't solely dependent on them. I finally knew I'd made it when I came to be referred to as the guy that made successful movies and wasn't identified by a particular project. It wasn't until I broke free from these limitations and started making my own mark that things changed. I was able to stay fresh and venture into TV with a diverse array of projects, like the remake of *Roots,* a doc titled *The Atlanta Child Murders,* and dating shows on OWN.

Staying in your lane does *not* mean limiting yourself. Your lane can be as wide as you define it to be. Own your lane. Make that your calling card, your hallmark. Part of owning your lane means making your area of expertise immediately identifiable as yours. Defining your personal brand. One of the most powerful things you can do is create a brand that people associate with both success and you personally. To do that, it needs to be clear what that brand represents, what it means, what it stands for. Consistently underscoring these is essential.

I've worked very hard to define my brand as a successful film and TV producer. People can say, "That guy produced the Oscars, that guy made *Girls Trip,* he's the one who's got successful reality shows." And that's what I was striving for, to be known by more than one thing. Over time, I've ventured into different genres, challenging the perception that I was only a specific genre guy. I realized that my success required me to break out of a single category or being constantly associated with someone else's name. It's about showcasing my abilities across the board. So yes, stay in your lane, but focus on the balance between that and showcasing your abilities within it. Embrace your multifaceted talents, seek growth, and continue to evolve while building success in a specific area. That's the definition of a wide lane.

"KEEP THE MAIN THING THE MAIN THING"

This simple but profound lesson comes from a friend of mine named Darrell Freeman, a remarkable individual who achieved great success in the business world but tragically took his own life. Darrell's close friend, DJ Wootson, gave a rousing tribute at his funeral and shared the invaluable advice Darrell would always impart: "Keep the main thing the main thing."

These words held great meaning for Darrell, both in business and in life. He knew the importance of staying focused on what truly mattered amid the distractions and pressures of the world. Darrell's success as a businessman and his incredible physical and mental endurance, exhibited in the fact that he completed multiple Ironman competitions, were a testament to his ability to prioritize and stay committed to his main goals.

However, somewhere along the way, he himself lost focus on the main thing. Heartbreakingly, the noise of life became deafening and he lost sight of what truly mattered, allowing other factors to overshadow the main thing in his life.

Reflecting on Darrell's story, I realized the significance of his words. When faced with disappointment, setbacks, or confusion, we must pause and ask ourselves, "Is this the main thing?" It's a powerful reminder to refocus our energies on what truly holds meaning and value in our lives.

Each of us has a unique main thing—an essential purpose or

goal that aligns with our values and brings us fulfillment. It may be nurturing our relationships, pursuing a passion, making a positive impact on others, or building a successful career. Whatever it may be, the main thing serves as our compass, guiding us through life's ups and downs.

However, staying true to the main thing requires discipline, self-awareness, and a constant reassessment of our priorities. We must resist the allure of distractions and the temptation to veer off course. It demands that we continuously evaluate our actions, ensuring they align with our core purpose in life.

So, let's embrace the wisdom of Darrell Freeman's mantra. Let us keep our main thing the main thing, grounding ourselves in its significance and holding it as our guiding light. Life can get really loud sometimes. The noise can be stressful and anxiety inducing. It can help to try to simplify our focus and not try to deal with or address everything that is vying for our attention. You know how when your smartphone battery starts to drain you should close as many windows as possible? Your mind works better when it can be focused as well. When faced with challenges, setbacks, or moments of doubt, let us remember to refocus, recommit, and realign our efforts with the main thing.

In doing so, we unlock the power to live a purpose-driven life, one that brings us fulfillment, joy, and a deep sense of accomplishment. By keeping the main thing at the forefront of our minds, we cultivate a sense of clarity, resilience, and unwavering determination. And in this journey, may we inspire others to discover and pursue their own main things, creating a ripple effect of purposeful living.

25

Spaceships Don't Come Equipped
with Rearview Mirrors

You Are Built for Forward Movement

You ever thought about how it's physically impossible to sit still on a bicycle? Sitting on an untethered bike and not pedaling is impossible unless you're a balancing wizard or have a stronger core than the Rock. Bicycles are engineered in such a way that you must be moving in order for them to work properly. Even if you're not going anywhere fast, you still gotta pedal. Thus, "riding a bike" and not "sitting a bike."

Humans are designed the same way. We are built to be moving, progressing. We break down when we're stagnant, so we always need to be moving forward. For me, personally, stagnation = total destruction. I promise I'm not being overly dramatic, although some might argue I've made a successful career dealing in overdramatizing. *{Narrator: He's being overly dramatic.}*

You know who agrees with me? André 3000. You know, the renowned flutist who used to rap? "Spaceships don't come equipped with rearview mirrors" is one of his best lyrics from "Int'l Players

Anthem." I can't write any more than that or we'll have to pay him a hefty royalty, and he doesn't need it with all the big wind instrument bank he's pulling in now. But basically, the vibe is that spaceships . . . *go*. They go to the moon, they go to the stars, they go into the future. It's not their purpose to be tethered to the ground, motionless. And certainly not to be looking back . . . at anything. No matter what's back there. You can't launch into the stratosphere looking rearward.

André and I, we don't look backward, we look forward. Even after I hit my tenth number-one movie with *Night School,* I couldn't help but keep my foot on the gas. It was a milestone worth celebrating, for sure—we rolled in some balloons and popped some champagne in our production office—but we didn't marinate in it for long. There were some "Woooooos!," maybe a few fist bumps and very unsexy A-frame hugs, then it was time to move on.

Our minds are engineered to move toward new goals, new accomplishments. Have you noticed that you just *feel* better when you're moving forward, working toward accomplishing something? Sometimes we have to trick our minds into thinking we're progressing for our own mental health. If you're stuck in a rut, don't stop moving forward. Even if it's just tiny increments of progress. You'll get out of it.

Let's say you're driving, and you hit a really bad storm with blinding rain. Experts don't advise just pulling over on the side of the freeway, stewing in your misery, and waiting for it to end. You don't know for sure what the storm is doing, and if it's not moving, now you're both just sitting there, potentially for hours. While you and that villainous storm are waiting for the other one to make a move, you're getting nowhere. Experts say keep moving, even if you're only going one mile per hour, even if there's no visibility. Keep inching forward a little bit at a time because you never know when you'll come out on the other side into the clear. In "Don't Quit," another of my favorite poems (after Rudyard Kipling's "If—"),

Edgar A. Guest implores, "Don't give up though the pace seems slow—you may succeed with another blow."

But, Will, I don't know which direction to go in. You're saying "move" and "go" and "progress," and all that sounds good, but how am I supposed to know the exact right way to do that? I hear you. When life is uncertain, be proactive. That's my go-to and it's served me well. I've had friends who were miserable in their jobs but were paralyzed with indecision and all they did was complain. I always told them the first thing they should do is clean up their résumés and send them out to their dream employers, because just the act of starting that process would put them in a better headspace. Progression, even if it's minuscule, still *feels* like progression. And that feels a lot better than stagnation, because eventually you're going to fall off that bike. Get to pedaling!

26

What Did You Think Was Going to Happen?

Be Careful What You Ask For

When I was in South Africa filming *Beast* (my man-eating lion movie starring Idris Elba), one day my wife, Heather; Ryan Engle (the writer of the movie); Jaime Primak Sullivan (our executive producer); and I went tracking in the bush. Now, while *tracking in the bush* kinda sounds like a new TikTok trend, it's actually more akin to a safari. The difference is typically when you go on safari in Africa, you're in touristy parks thirty minutes outside of major cities where the animals are used to humans. You follow the well-worn tracks of the hundred thousand jeeps that have done the same trails before, and the wildlife poses with you for selfies. It's slightly more exotic than being at the zoo. Tracking is when you go looking for animals that you have to go to extremes to find. Animals that probably don't want to be found.

We shot much of *Beast* deep in the South African bush, five hours from the closest major city. We were so far out, somebody could shoot you and they might never find your body. And that actually did happen sometimes in the bush. It was that remote. The South African bush could be a scary and dangerous place. But being Will Packer, I had to try tracking, as Will Packer is wont to do. *{Narrator: Debatable choice to go third person here, but I'll allow it.}*

So, we're out there in an open-air Range Rover–type thing, plowing through very rough bush, tracking our fool heads off, driving over rocks and mud pits, trying not to get stuck. There's no AAA in the bush. There are, however, giraffes and leopards and rhinos, all of which we saw with the help of our two expert conservationists. One of the experts would go right up to a giant pile of dung, stick his face inches from it, inhale deeply, and relay excitedly, "The rhinos are close by! It's still warm!" We followed the poo path and, sure enough, were able to see an endangered white rhino calf and her mother. I thought two things: One—"Wow, this guy is good!" And two—"I probably won't talk too closely to him for the rest of the trip."

The main prize we were tracking was herds of wild elephants, some of which had been tagged with transmitters. The guides had a primitive tracking device that looked like a ham radio with a bent antenna. I was expecting more of an iPad with a digital map, but that was not the case. The radio made a not-so-subtle beeping sound. The closer together the beeps of the machine, the closer we were to the elephants.

As the sun began to set, we were bummed we might not see them. We had been at it for four hours and had seen some really cool wildlife, but no elephants. Oh well, maybe next time. But right then we heard "dee dee dee deee deeee" on the wonky radio-walkie thingamabob. We got a hit. We followed the beeps deeper into the bush, rolling over mounds of boulders and tree stumps. I was definitely apprehensive about how far we were going into the rough terrain, but I figured anybody that can detect the proximity of rhinos from the scent of droppings must know what they're doing. The truck came to a halt, and, at first, I was afraid he'd gotten lost and we might be stuck miles from civilization as darkness fell.

"Wait," our expert whispered. "Shhhh, listen, listen." We heard branches cracking off in the distance. Suddenly, about five hundred feet in front of us, the most incredible herd of elephants came into view. We had finally found them. It was an exhilarating sight to behold, made even more magnificent by the fact that they were truly in their natural habitat. The first thing that struck me was that these elephants were *way* bigger than I was prepared for. We were sitting on top of this open-air truck, and it was like looking up at a two-story building. The biggest female elephant, the matriarch, was leading the way as these majestic beasts lumbered behind her. It was magical.

"I'm gonna try to get a little bit closer," the guide said quietly.

I'm thinking, "You really don't have to. We can see them just fine from here."

As soon as we crept a few feet forward, a young bull elephant near the back of the pack turned and looked straight at us. Uh-oh.

The guide explained that young bull elephants are always trying to prove their worth, so they can be hostile. Especially when they are in musth. Musth is when a bull elephant's testosterone and reproductive hormone levels are surging. Similar to when a female animal is in heat. Musth causes the males to be uncharacteristically aggressive. As he was explaining this, the young bull was starting to head toward us. "Be very quiet. This one is in musth!" the guide said excitedly.

I have no idea why the guide was excited because we certainly weren't. Just when Heather, Jaime, Ryan, and I reached consensus that we had seen enough of the bush and now would probably be a good time to start heading back, the bull elephant started to charge us. We gasped collectively. Heather grabbed my thigh and started squeezing.

An elephant doesn't charge at you as much as they *stomp* toward you. On account of their size, every step is thunderous. As he approached he was shaking his head and intentionally knocking over whole trees. It was explained that this is typical behavior for an animal in his state. He was displaying his strength in the only juvenile way he knew how. He had all this testosterone coursing through his veins because he was still too young to get any loving from the ladies in the herd. He hadn't earned his way high enough in the pecking order to get any premium elephant tail and he was *not* happy about it.

He was bowing up, knocking over trees, and stomping around with his giant elephant penis swinging around, gallons of pee spraying everywhere. Every adult human male should have to experience a bull elephant in musth. I promise you it would take us all down a few notches. We don't have shit to brag about. On any level. I will never forget the pungent smell of elephant urine. It was easily the most abhorrent thing I've ever had the displeasure of smelling in my life, and it was just constantly running down his leg the whole time. The entire spectacle was horrifying.

Now, we are all ready to get the eff up outta there. But here's the thing: We were so deep in the bush that we couldn't just turn around and hightail it. There were so many rocks and trees that we couldn't have driven away fast enough. And us fleeing would've just enraged him further and encouraged him to give chase. The elephant would catch us and trample us like a matchbox car. By now this stomping, peeing, angry creature was close enough that I could see mucus coming out of its eyes. That's when our guide did the unthinkable. He drove *toward* the elephant, revving the engine really loud. The bull stopped in his tracks and even backed up a couple feet. When he backed up, so did we. Then the bull stomped toward us again. Now we were in this weird back-and-forth dance. Every time he charged, our driver revved the engine, and the elephant would stop and back up a couple paces. Then he would charge us again. This went on for what felt like an eternity. And although we were trying to back up as much as we could, we could only do so a few feet at a time, and each time the young bull was getting closer and closer. I looked back and still couldn't see a clear path out of the bush, and this elephant would not stop coming. He was *pissed*. I can't remember being so terrified. I'm pretty sure I had pee running down my leg too.

The whole time this is going on we are all holding our breaths, trying not to make a sound. I took my phone out, but not to take a video; I wrote a note to my kids saying goodbye. I hoped my will was in order. I could not see getting out of this situation alive. I looked over at Jaime. She was silently and uncontrollably sobbing. Tears streaming down both cheeks. I looked down and realized there was blood on my thigh. It was my blood. Heather was so scared that she had dug her nails into my leg and broken the skin through my pants. I hadn't even noticed. Ryan, the writer, was staring at the elephant in wide-eyed amazement. "This is so fascinating!" he whispered. Writers are weird.

The elephant was still knocking over trees angrily. We couldn't go anywhere. Our driver was backing up and going forward and backing up and going forward. One time he backed up into a tree behind us, and I said aloud, "Oh God, this is it. This is how it ends."

These elephants were minding their business, and we did the most dumb human thing of all. We tracked them for hours, and we found them in their habitat. We were not satisfied and got closer. Did we think that when we finally found them, they would be behind glass and we could stick a quarter in a machine and get peanuts to feed them? That the elephants would be like, "Wow! You found us! Want to make a reel for Instagram?"

No, this elephant did what elephants sometimes do. Charge at dumbass humans. It was literally an hour before we somehow backed far enough away to be able to turn around and get the heck out of there. Thank you, God. I had a funny thought as we drove back to our base camp in the cold African darkness in complete silence: "What the hell did we think was going to happen?"

There is a very straightforward lesson here. In the vein of being careful what you ask for, always be sure that you're prepared for the end result of a path you choose to go down. As you strategize around the many decisions you are making in your life, don't be surprised when a plausible outcome actually comes to fruition. Said another way: If you're going to act all big and bad, you better be ready to deal with a well-hung bull. Apply that as you will.

27

The Best Time to Plant a Tree

Don't Obsess About How Far Behind You Are; Start Catching Up Today

There is an old proverb that says, "The best time to plant a tree is twenty years ago. The second-best time? Today."

The world's POV shifted in the summer of 2020 after George Floyd was murdered by the police. Protesters hit the streets, the Black Lives Matter movement surged, and it's also when I like to say that many white people woke up and realized they were white and what that meant to nonwhite people. "Oh my God, this is something that white people actually do? Like historically?! We're horrible!"

All that rampant Black anger and white guilt resulted in many companies taking a closer look at their own cultures, hiring practices, and diversity. Whether they were ultimately doing this because of their bottom line or because they actually wanted to do better is up for debate. But a lot of companies, especially in Hollywood and the media, felt they needed to bring in a nonwhite person to talk to their employees. I was asked a bunch of times to come in to talk at companies' town halls. We were all feeling angst, but I didn't feel it was a good use of the moment to just tear into the audience about how awful they and their employers had been. Here was a moment where many white people were seemingly actually open to listening and maybe even changing. I chose to try to help them see how they could do and be better going forward.

I told them, "Don't be ashamed of being born on second base, but don't brag about hitting a double. When you see a kid on first base, understand the impact of your privilege on the metaphorical baseball game. Doesn't mean you did something wrong to anyone else, but be honest about the entitlement that you have and the positions you have been fortunate to be placed in."

Many white Hollywood executives reached out during this time to help them staff their companies with Black talent. "I need more diversity," they said. "I know I [bleeped] up in not doing it sooner, but I'm ready now. I need a high-ranking Black executive to run my blah blah blah department." I would listen patiently, staring at them like you might stare at a petulant child on a road trip in the middle of nowhere who is demanding ice cream. My company had been doing that for a decade already—our film crews were not only full of people of color, but we've also always made it a point to champion women directors and writers too. But bragging about that in the moment would serve no greater purpose, not if I wanted to help be part of the solution, and I did.

The first thing I had to explain was that it doesn't work like that. You can't just *poof* have high-ranking Black executives appear magically out of thin air. They're not AI robots (yet) to be created overnight. They have to be mentored and nurtured. Here's a fitting analogy: Right as Covid restrictions were ending and everything was opening back up, I was in Las Vegas for a birthday party. One of the casino concierges told me they had almost zero inventory of top-shelf alcohol because everything had sold out as soon as people were allowed to travel again. That combined with major delays in the supply chain meant really high-end liquor was scarce. Didn't matter. Soon after this casino sold out of their last bottle of a popular twenty-year-old scotch, a high roller came in and demanded a bottle, boasting, "I'll pay fifty thousand dollars for the bottle."

"You don't understand," the concierge told him. "I can't sell it to you. It doesn't exist. It literally takes twenty years to make."

The point is, these companies didn't have Black executives who were waiting in the wings primed to take positions of power, just like the casino didn't have that twenty-year-old scotch, because they didn't invest in them two decades ago. They never adequately hired and trained Black employees for upper-level management positions, so there was little inventory to choose from during the tumultuous summer of 2020. You can't just mold high-level Black executives out of clay because now you need them.

I explained how they needed to start hiring that BIPOC person now as an intern to level up to an assistant to level up to a junior executive associate to level up to a senior-level executive. You must invest in young BIPOC people today, be serious and focused on their advancement, and then twenty years from now you'll have your high-ranking, talented BIPOC executives. But the time to start is five minutes ago. This applies to improving your business or personal situation across the board.

Start doing the work now so that you're in a better position at this same time tomorrow. If we're talking about tolerance or diversity within your organization, bring in people from marginalized communities who aren't in your company. Bring them in now at various levels so in due time, they can reach the top. Start an intern program, bring in kids from HBCUs, bring in kids from inner cities and Latino communities. Start now because you'll benefit from it later. Don't obsess about how far behind you are. That's okay. One foot in front of the other.

Now, as I've risen up the ranks of Hollywood, I have seen more and more Black content being made because it has started to make undeniable amounts of money. I'm proud that my box-office track record has contributed to that. It's clear there is a global appetite for more of these authentic stories. You are definitely seeing more Black, Latino, Asian, Native American, and LGBTQ stories being told by Hollywood, but remember we were so far behind as an industry to begin with that progress is relative. I'm also still not seeing those people represented at the highest rungs of power. Not in a substantive way. During the major Hollywood actors' and writers' strike in 2023, almost all the heads of the studios at the negotiating table were straight white men. There was one woman: Donna Langley from Universal, who, by the way, is a powerhouse of an executive who can hold her own in any room and is one of my strongest relationships in the biz.

With the cyclical ebb and flow of social justice prioritization, many companies pulled back from diversity promises made during that very hot-button time. That's why the most effective strategy isn't one driven by the cultural heat of a particular moment, but rather understanding that in bottom-line businesses your bottom line is made better by extremely talented individuals with a diversity of backgrounds and perspectives. So, if you didn't plant the tree twenty years ago, the next best time is *today*. Like I tell many of my white colleagues, it's never too late and intentionality matters. I applaud your intentions. And next time you win a "race" in some aspect of life, take a look at where you started from before announcing how great you are.

28

Good Things Come to Those Who Grind

Sometimes You Just Gotta Rise Up

We're all running this race called Life, and no matter whether the day is a sprint or a marathon, the advice my high school track coach, Coach Ken Jackson, gave me holds true. He would always say, "Packer, keep your head down. At the start of the race, don't worry about the finish line. That's got nothing to do with you. If you don't focus on what's right in front of you, you'll never make it way down to the finish line anyway." I've taken all that to heart. While I'm a dreamer who's always had lofty goals and aspirations, I've found success by focusing on the thing in front of me. I'm a believer in the idea that when you work hard and put yourself in a position to succeed, good things will happen. As you put the work in and do things the right way, people will take notice. You may end up in fortuitous situations that you didn't even see coming. I'm a living example of that.

On May 21, 2024, one of my biggest dreams became a reality when thirty-two National Football League owners voted unanimously to approve three others and myself as the new limited partners of the

NFL's Atlanta Falcons ownership group. I did not see this coming. To give this some context, let's start by recognizing that NFL ownership has traditionally been, and continues to be, one of the most exclusive clubs in the world. You probably have a better chance of getting struck by lightning while cashing in a winning lottery ticket.

Remember ride-or-die Shayla? She of the oranges under the freeway overpass? Shayla has always been a great connector. She came to me one day in 2023 and said one of her contacts who had worked in the Obama White House had an investment opportunity I might want to consider. My eyes glazed over because I'm always hearing about "opportunities." Most times said opportunity benefits only the person offering it, while making my bank account lighter. It's one of the hazards of success. You have to be constantly wary of what people are asking of you. One of my celebrity friends says that when they are talking to people, they just count down for "the ask." Meaning there's never any organic conversations. It goes something like this:

"Hey, Maddie, what are you doing here? I haven't seen you since high school!"

"I know, right?! So great to see you too, Will."

3 . . . 2 . . . 1 . . .

"Hey, I got this script I'd love for you to read . . ." *Bam.*

"Hey, I have a nephew who wants to act, and I need you to take a look at . . ." *Bam.*

"Hey, I could really use your help, I'm about to lose my house . . ." *Bummer.* And *Bam.*

So as Shayla's starting to explain this so-called investment opportunity, my eyes are rolling into the back of my brain, and she can sense it so she gets right to the punch line: "I wouldn't even bring it to you, but it's the NFL." Record scratch. DJ, take it to the bridge. Say *whut.*

What do you mean, the NFL? The National *Foosball* League? The Norwegian French Fry Legion? There's only one NFL that matters. You can't be talking about that one. It sounded too good to be true, like my strip club cleaning business. Turns out it was *very* legit. Shayla knew a guy who knew a guy who was putting together a group of minority (meaning stake *and* POC) shareholders to be considered by the Atlanta Falcons. Their motto is Rise Up. This is the team I *rose up* for and trash-talked my way into almost getting a beer thrown at my head during Super Bowl LI. Were they ready to reciprocate the loyalty?

Derrick Heggans, the Black businessman who was organizing this group of potential new NFL minority owners, was former in-house counsel for the NFL and had gone around to various owners to ask, "If I can put together a group of successful African Americans, would you be interested in bringing new limited partners into your franchise?" Arthur Blank, owner of the Atlanta Falcons, had in fact been considering bringing on additional limited partners. NFL limited partners are sometimes referred to as minority owners. They are investors in the franchise and typically have a passive role in the actual operation of the team. But we have established that I'm one hell of a fantasy football coach, so just in case they need ideas on fourth down, I'm here. *{Narrator: There will be absolutely no calling fourth-down plays for Mr. Packer. Thank God.}* The timing worked out such that all my work in the film industry and the Atlanta community was about to coincide with the opportunity of a lifetime. I was on the short list. As we've discussed, it only takes one strategically placed white guy, right?

Another one of the good guys in the billionaire ranks is Tony Ressler, co-founder of private equity firms Ares Management and Apollo Global Management, and owner of the NBA's Atlanta Hawks. He owns the Hawks with his wife, actress Jami Gertz. Tony, Jami, Heather, and I are fast friends. One of my favorite stories Tony tells is how when he bought the Hawks, he was told by his L.A. friends, "There are three people you must meet in Atlanta: [then-] Mayor Kasim Reed, Ambassador Andrew Young, and Will Packer." To which Tony replied immediately, "Who the #$%* is Will

Packer?" He told me that story at our first couples' dinner, and we've been close ever since. He asked me to join the board of the Atlanta Hawks Foundation and included me on his investment team for a major development project in downtown Atlanta. Let's just say that Tony Ressler and Arthur Blank know the right time to plant a tree.

Once Heather and I discussed the opportunity (and came to grips with the fact that, if we were successful, our days of cheering for the Bucs and Cowboys were numbered), we decided we were all in. That began an extremely arduous process of financial vetting, background checking, and high-level approvals—first at the team level with Arthur Blank and Co. and then at the NFL level. I can't go into much detail, but suffice to say the process is no joke. The NFL is the most valuable sports league in the world and is understandably very protective of its image and who they allow into its ownership ranks. For eight months I was subjected to a proceeding that I had very little control over. I was asked about financial decisions and speeding tickets that were over ten years old. I was asked about social media posts I had "engaged" with that were older than that. {*Narrator: Be careful what you "like" online, ladies and gents. Someone's always watching.*} As with any such process, I was asked to provide references. I brought out the big guns. They know who they are, and I'm extremely thankful for them. The group being considered was always small, but with each stage of the process, as we got closer to final approval, the group got smaller and smaller. I kept worrying they were going to find out about the time Eric had weed in my mom's minivan. I had my whole "upstanding citizen" speech ready to go. Somehow, I continued to make the cut.

About a year after beginning my unlikely journey to the ranks of NFL ownership, I was at a business lunch in L.A. when I saw a number come up on my phone that I recognized as *the* number I was waiting to hear from. This was it. The answer on whether I got the final approval or not. Taking a cue from my homie Rudyard Kipling, I did not run out of the restaurant with my napkin in my shirt collar to take the call. That would have been a little desperate, not to mention rude. The people I was dining with deserved my full attention. Whatever triumph or disaster was on that call would have to wait. Never get too high or too low. It was either the greatest news or the worst, and I didn't want to risk getting crushing news in the middle of lunch anyway. If I had the cajones to tell Sony Pictures that Will Packer was in meetings all morning while sitting around in my boxer shorts, surely I had the intestinal fortitude to say, "Whatever the outcome is, you, Will Packer, have no control over it. Stay focused. Compartmentalize." It's not easy to do, but I'm blessed to have that skill.

At the end of the lunch, I took a deep breath, called back, and got the news that it was unanimous. The entire group passed. I was officially approved to be a limited partner of the Atlanta Falcons. *Rise the *bleep* up*!

Corporate titan Rosalind Brewer, Olympic gold medalist Dominique Dawes, and venture capitalist Rashaun Williams were the other three selected. Two women, two men, three HBCU grads, all successful African Americans.

I've told you how every day can be your birthday. Well, in this case this endeavor actually did line up with a milestone birthday of mine. I knew that if I got approved it would happen around my fiftieth birthday. I couldn't think of a better way to celebrate a half century on this earth. Friends kept asking me what I was doing for my fiftieth, thinking I would say I was planning a major party in some exotic locale. I would simply say, "I've got something else in mind." The timing worked out, and I was able to announce on social media that I was giving myself the birthday gift of a lifetime.

When I think about what this means, I think about how representation matters. I think about how when I go into communities, schools, and corporations now, I do so not just as Will Packer, successful film and television producer, but also as an ambassador for the Atlanta Falcons. I think about how the next generation of Black kids can see someone who looks like them and realize they don't have to be an elite athlete or entertainer to excel at the highest levels.

I also think about the proud Packer legacy I am continuing. I think about my grandfather standing up to Klan members in Alabama and my father being the first Black engineering graduate at his university. I think about my mom telling me B's were just fine but I could always do better. I think about my children, grandchildren, and great-grandchildren inheriting my stake and creating generational wealth. *{Narrator: He's joking; it's all going to Suki.}* As I've encouraged you to, I set my own bar for success. It was a very high bar, and I've faced big challenges along the way, some seemingly insurmountable. It will be the same for you. But if you don't keep pushing forward despite overwhelming odds, you may not be in position to take advantage when your limited-partner-of-the-Atlanta-Falcons opportunity comes knocking. Be ready; there are always going to be bumps and challenges and ups and downs and things that you don't account for anytime you take a risk and dream big. You define success for yourself, not somebody else. I've been blessed to accomplish so much of what I set out to do and then some. With NFL ownership, I made my lane just a little bit wider.

Some days I look at all I've accomplished and think I'm living a dream, then I remember how hard I worked to make this dream my reality. I realize it's not luck or happenstance but rather the cumulative effect of putting myself in a favorable position by working my ass off.

I gave a quote that was included in the Atlanta Falcons press release announcing our approval as limited partners. It read:

> The power of representation and equity should never be underestimated, and as someone who has dedicated his career to creating diverse imagery, I have a true appreciation of Mr. Blank's commitment to opening doors that have historically been closed to African Americans. This investment

represents not only the personal opportunity of a lifetime, but also the chance to demonstrate for generations to come that someone who looks like me can excel not only on the field, but at the highest level of the exclusive ranks of NFL ownership.

Period.

{Narrator: Good thing the NFL never discovered you still *haven't won your fantasy football league championship, huh?}*

Shut up, Narrator.

29

Drive the Benz!

Get Busy Living

We've all heard some version of the advice that we should appreciate the blessings in our life today because tomorrow is not guaranteed. I'm a firm believer that if you're always playing it safe, following all the rules, and being a responsible adult 24/7, well, you're missing out on the good stuff. Let me explain where my philosophy comes from.

It began on December 31, 2007, when I received a life-altering call from my mother. I was at home in Atlanta having a low-key New Year's Eve. I remember reflecting on the year that had been and the year that was ahead. Like many of us around that time, I was excited about the potential of new beginnings and changes that were to come. My mind was on leaving the old behind and embarking on my own personal next chapter. All that changed when the phone rang shortly before midnight.

My father had suffered a major heart attack and was fighting for his life in the hospital in Florida. My younger sister, Tameche, who was pregnant at the time, was already there because she was spending the holidays with my parents. "You should get here," Mom said. "They don't know if he's going to make it through the night." I booked the first flight I could and boarded a plane the next morning from Atlanta to St. Pete, praying fervently for his recovery.

God, if it be your will, please allow Pops to recover from this. And if nothing else, please just allow me to see him one last time on this earth.

Arriving at the hospital, I was relieved to find my father still alive, though tenuously holding on to life. He was on a breathing machine and had coded twice overnight. But each time he came back. When I got there, he was holding on. I was able to have some time with him. Just him and me in his hospital room together. He had held on until I arrived, then shortly after I walked out of the room he passed away. January 1, 2008. I'll be forever thankful we got to have that moment. If you've experienced the loss of a close loved one, you know that everything becomes a blur of arrangements, condolences, and things that need to get done. My mom was in major mourning. My pregnant sister needed to be sure she was taking care of herself and her baby. Our patriarch was gone. I tried to step into the void as best I could.

When my dad passed I was just about to start pre-production on *Obsessed,* featuring the now firmly committed Beyoncé and Idris Elba. It helped to be busy, to have something that required a ton of my attention. In April of that year, while I was shooting on a soundstage at Sony Pictures in Culver City, California, unbelievably I got yet another terrifying call from my mom. My sister Tameche had just been in a horrific car accident in Atlanta. It was bad. She had been rushed to the hospital. She was six months pregnant. They weren't sure whether she or the baby would make it. Dear God, not again.

I got on the next flight from L.A. to Atlanta and just started praying. *Dear Lord. Please, please, please spare my sister and her baby. Please allow them to pull through.*

This was when there was no Internet on planes. The four-plus-hour flight from LAX to ATL felt endless. I was disconnected from the world and in the dark the whole time. Still raw from my dad's death, I had no idea what I would be arriving to when I landed. When we finally touched down, I found out that after very extensive surgery they were able to save my sister and the baby. But my sister would have a very long road to physical recovery, and the baby, born three months prematurely, had brain damage.

Miracle, as my sister aptly named her little girl, became a cherished part of our lives. She was diagnosed with cerebral palsy and will never be verbal or have advanced development. Her special needs require constant unwavering love and support. I can't think of a more perfect mother who has the right amount of patience, perseverance, and mama bear energy than my sister. She and Miracle go everywhere. Movies, plays, amusement parks, bowling, international trips, you name it. Tameche makes sure that Miracle lives an incredibly full life. Though we'd encountered severe unexpected challenges, we embraced Miracle's presence and thanked God for her survival. We celebrated each day as a gift and learned to appreciate the small miracles that brought us together.

These consecutive moments of trauma forever changed my perspective on life. I had always been a driven and determined individual, focused on achieving success in my career. However, the loss of my father and the accident involving my sister taught me the fragility of life and the importance of gratitude. In many ways Tameche and I have a typical brother-sister relationship. We lovingly rib each other all the time. I first learned to crack jokes on people by going back and forth with her growing up. The surgery from the accident left her with many scars and a permanent pin in her hip that causes her to walk with a slight limp.

"Lord, I ain't ever gonna hear the end of this from you!" I remember her saying about the limp.

I said, "That's the most beautiful limp ever. Because it reminds me that I still have you."

I thank God for deciding not to take my dad, my sister, and

my niece in the same year. I'm grateful for Tameche's resilience and our unbreakable bond. I treasure the presence of Miracle, who through her very existence teaches me the true meaning of unconditional love and acceptance.

Life's unexpected twists and turns have shaped me into the person I am today—a storyteller, a survivor, and a believer in the power of embracing life's wonders. That season of my life also taught me the value of taking a moment to pause, breathe, and appreciate my blessings. I realized there are things that are completely out of our control and that tomorrow is never guaranteed.

I feel like there are two Wills: the one before this all happened and the one after. As I grew more successful after 2008, the accomplishments meant more. They tasted different, better, more meaningful. In some ways I grew more cautious and hesitant in my life. I think I was fearful because I had seen how in an instant things can change. But I think that was me missing one of the main lessons.

My first major success by Hollywood standards was *Stomp the Yard.* It was a box-office hit by any measure, and I decided to splurge on my first luxury car. I bought a 2007 pearl-white S600 Mercedes-Benz. That car became my pride and joy. I kept it in pristine condition and would only drive it sparingly. Five years after I bought that car, I was so proud to only have thirteen thousand miles on it. I went to see my accountant at the time, Barren Watson, and as we were going over liabilities and assets I was beaming, telling him about my mint-condition Benz. His reaction surprised me. "Why?" he admonished. "For what? As soon as you took it off the lot it depreciated. There's no real value in that car. What are you saving it for? You plan to sell it as a vintage Mercedes someday? Its primary value is to you right now. Drive the Benz. Enjoy it!"

He was so right. And now I dole out the same advice. I have a buddy who, at one point, had almost a million saved Delta Sky-

Miles. This guy is conservative. A saver. When he told me, I was like, "What are you saving them for? Use the miles! See the world!"

When I get airline miles, I use them, usually right away. I fly like crazy and I've already used more miles than most people will see in a lifetime. But as soon as I get them, I use them on the next trip. I think you should too. If you have something very specific to save for, fine. If you need to save up a hundred thousand miles to go to Europe next summer, great. But generally speaking, today's the rainy day. Use it or lose it.

You gotta live life like that because it can turn on a dime.

Take that spontaneous trip, indulge in that guilty pleasure, have the dessert even when you've been hitting the gym. Buy the expensive shoes every now and then—who cares if you can't afford them? Screw it, buy them anyway! Your inner fashionista deserves to shine. Life is about balance, but sometimes you must let loose and have a damn good time. Don't forget to sprinkle some madness and excitement into your journey. Embrace your wild side and live a life that's worth every laughter-filled, adventure-packed moment. Because when you look back, it's those moments of pure joy and spontaneity that will bring the biggest smiles to your face. So go ahead, take risks, make some mistakes, and create memories that'll make your grandkids question your sanity. Trust me, tomorrow is not promised.

EPILOGUE

Leave a Legacy

You have been building your own personal legacy for as long as you've been alive. You are the cumulative effect of your decisions, actions, and efforts. You've made some mistakes and you've also made some great choices. If you take to heart a lot of the things I'm suggesting in this book, you will be proud of the legacy you leave behind. I promise you.

My HBCU college experience is so important to me; it shaped me into the man I am today. It's where I found my voice and learned to tell stories. In 2021, Florida A&M University unveiled the Will Packer Performing Arts Amphitheater. It was one of the most profoundly moving days of my life. We made sure to do it really big. Famed broadcaster Stephen A. Smith brought First Take and ESPN to broadcast live. Various celebs showed up to support. Kevin Hart made a cross-country trip to show love. Taraji P. Henson, Chris Paul, and Idris Elba sent video congratulations. We had a huge custom float in the parade. We did all the things. To have my name on a building at my beloved alma mater is as cool as you would imagine it to be. It's also phenomenally humbling and confirmation of a life well lived. I jokingly said after the unveiling, "My work on this earth is done."

Who would have ever thunk it? I wanted to go to an Ivy League school, but FAMU gave me a full ride and my parents said, "We love you, son. We support your independence. We're proud you got accepted into an Ivy. But you are going to Florida A&M." Thank you, Mom. Thank you, Dad.

My legacy is not how many number-one movies I have; it's how many people I've influenced, who then go on to have their own "number ones."

The thing I want to be remembered by is the impact on the people I have affected. Think about that when you focus on the things you want to accomplish on the road to success. If you take nothing else from this book, take the fact that everything is about perspective, and the prism through which you view success will affect the way that you achieve said success. Think not just in terms of your own individual or material accomplishments but in terms of your impact on your family, those closest to you, your community, even the global community. What you leave behind and the people you impact will make your accomplishments much more powerful and enduring.

I'm as proud of the fact that I have former interns who went on to make their own movies, run their own shows, and win Academy Awards as I am of the things that I've achieved myself. It's just as powerful when you pay it forward, because hopefully the person you impacted impacts somebody else. If I win, that's one win. But if I help you win and I leave you with a mentality of how to help others win, well, that might be ten wins, a hundred wins. We like to win, you and me. We're winners. But nothing's better than maximizing our wins by creating other winners.

Success for me isn't about a list of accomplishments I can rattle off. It's about the happiness that it brings. I've tried so hard to protect my joy throughout my career. I've got ten number-one movies so far. If I could have twenty but not be as happy, I don't want them. If I could only have five and be happier, gimme the five. For some people, achievement and success is what drives their joy. I can relate, but there's always a point where the drive for success and achievement takes away from the joy. And that's the tipping point that you don't want to go past.

Shayla and I laugh at how she is always trying to get me to show up to big Hollywood events that are packed with influential people. "You need to be in these rooms!" she'll say. She knows often I couldn't care less. It's true that I worked this hard in part so I could be invited to the hot Hollywood party. But I also worked this hard so I could have the option to *not* go to the hot Hollywood party.

If I got into this industry for the fame and elbow-rubbing of it all, I wouldn't be as successful as I am. I try to keep a very clear balance in my life. I encourage you to do the same. I have had pinch-me moments where I finally allowed myself to just soak up and breathe in all I've been blessed to accomplish. The announcement of my Atlanta Falcons investment was definitely one of those moments. But me being me, of course I have no intention of stopping anytime soon. There are more worlds to conquer.

My advice for how you keep going? Continue to redefine success. The world is always changing, so our definition of success has to keep changing. I believe in perpetual progression. Always moving. Even if sometimes it feels like I'm not moving forward. Even if I'm in quicksand, if my legs are moving at least I'm trying.

Heather often asks me if there is something I want to do after the film industry. I jokingly tell her I'm considering politics. Maybe mayor of my hometown, St. Petersburg, Florida? She immediately vetoes me: "No way. I don't want that life and neither do you."

There's a rinky-dink little strip club in St. Pete Beach not far from where I grew up, called Mermaids. As a playful threat I tell her, "Listen, when I'm done with Hollywood, I'm either going to be mayor of St. Pete or I can be a strip club owner. Can't do both. It's your choice."

I get the same answer every time: "Go buy Mermaids."

LASTLY

Put Your Head Down and Strive

A decade after I became a successful movie producer, the one, the only Oprah invited me to her majestic Montecito, California, estate, aptly named Promised Land, to talk about collaborating for her network OWN. *{Narrator: All roads lead back to Oprah.}* As we toured the grounds in her golf cart, she told me how when she was rising up, all she ever wanted was six trees in her yard. She grew up dirt poor in a wood-frame shack in Mississippi. Her neighbor had three stately trees, and Oprah would just stare at them in wonder. She made it her goal to have twice as many trees as her neighbor one day.

Oprah said she put her head down and "worked and worked and worked," then, pointing to the gorgeous endless avocado orchard on her forty-two-acre property, she added, "Now I've got a forest." She wanted a mere six trees and ended up with a national park in her front yard. If that's not a testament to the power of setting a goal, working your butt off to achieve it, and, before you know it, surpassing it, I don't know what is.

As we stood there and I stared at her thousands of trees, I thought about my journey and how my own relentless grind had led me to building my own small "forest." I thought about how when you block out the noise and focus on the work, you can end up with success beyond even your own expectations.

As she walked away I continued to gaze out at the fruits of her labor, and I was just left with one final thought: "Why didn't you come to my *Chocolate City* premiere?"

ACKNOWLEDGMENTS

I'm about to take y'all to church like a hard-core rapper at an awards show in the early 2000s: first and foremost, giving honor and glory to God, the most high, who is the center of my life and who has carried me through the most incredible highs and challenging lows. Thank you, Jesus. Let the church say "Amen."

This book was a labor of love. I'm so appreciative of the many people who have been instrumental in getting me to this point. I'm the cumulative result of an unmatched village's support. HP, you already know. Till the wheels fall off. You are my entire world. I'll spend my life trying (and failing) to show you how much you mean to me. Gramms! Thank you and Pops for raising me to be fearless, proud, and confident. You made me what I am. I've tried to instill those same traits in my brood. Dom Diesel, Nija P, Z-Packy, MP! Y'all are the reason. Period. Read that again. I love y'all more than you'll ever know. Keep showing them your greatness.

Tameche, you're the strongest person I know and also the blackest bump. Love you. Shay-Shay! We did it man. What's next? Whatever it is we'll take it on together and it doesn't stand a chance. Six Neener, what's understood doesn't need to be said. You already know. Till the wheels fall off.

To the institution that was so vital to my development, THE Florida A&M University, thank you. I didn't know me before I met you. Robbie D, thank you for having the initial dream and opening my mind to what was possible and always supporting your brother. The Beta Nu chapter of Alpha Phi Alpha Fraternity, Inc. Osirians! Dharvy! Love you, Sis. St. Pete High School.

All the amazing casts I've worked with. Kev Hart, love you, boy. Regina Hall, where Biddy at?! Love you, boo. Big Drister, all luv, bruv. Timmy, Mally Mal, Tina G . . . thanks for making me look smart. KP, I never would've graduated without you! Queen D, you are one of one. Thank you for being you. Clint! I wouldn't be where I am without you. Thank you for teaching me so, so, so much. ValQ, yo mama! Love you, cuz.

Coach Wiz, thank you for teaching me the power of self-belief. Steve Harvey, hope I'm still making you proud, Unk. Regina Brooks, thanks for putting me on game in an industry I knew very little about. Matthew Benjamin, what you think, MB? Hope I made you look smart. The entire marketing, sales, and editorial team at Penguin Random House—Who Better Than Y'all?

My WPP and WPM teams, y'all keep me upright and make me look good. Thank you. The entire team at Collective Edge Management, thank you for putting me in position to win.

Tony Ressler and Jami Gertz, thank you for being incredible human beings. Arthur Blank, thank you for leaning in when it would have been much safer not to. I'm forever grateful.

My incredible Exumian family—I'm on the way!

Dibs! What you think? Think we got one? Yeah . . . me too. Forever indebted. Thank you.

INDEX

Hudlin, Warrington, 64, 125, 147, 179

Ice Cube, xii, 4, 132, 197
"If—" (Kipling), 85, 206, 222, 223
Inception (film), 27

Jackson, Ken, 219
Jay-Z, 7, 8, 151–52
Jeezy, 18, 97
Jobs, Steve, 143
Jordan, Michael, 169
joy, 183
    greatness and, 107
    leaning in and, 166
    perspective and, 234–35
"Just Like Candy" (song), 131, 135

King, Martin Luther, Jr., 86
    Memorial in Washington, 91, 92
Kipling, Rudyard, 85, 206, 222

Lady of Rage, 147
Langley, Donna, 218
Lawrence, Martin, 190
lean into your thing, 199–203
    choosing a career and, 164–66
    definition of a wide lane, 202
    focus and, 203
    Freeman's story and, 202–3
    mantra, "keep the main thing the
        main thing," 200, 202–3
    not limiting yourself and, 201
    personal branding and, 201
    purposeful living and, 203
    Will playing high school football
        and, 199–200
Lee, Spike, 125
legacy, 233–35
Let Me Explain (Hart's comedy
    special), 7–12, 134
Lett, Leon, 15–16
life/living in the moment, 227–31
    importance of gratitude, 229–30

lesson: drive the Benz, 230
lesson: use airline miles, 230–31
tomorrow not promised, 227, 231
trauma and perspective, 229
Will's father's death, 227–28
Will's sister's accident, 228–30
Lopez, Jennifer, 7
"Lost One" (song), 151–52
Lovett, Richard, 65
Ludacris, 18, 39, 190
Luessenhop, John, 80

Malco, Romany, 29
Mason, Skip, 91
Micheaux, Oscar, 125
Miles, Moses General, 124–25
MLK Memorial Foundation, Leaders
    of Democracy Awards, 91

Nard, 156, 157
"Neighbors" (song), 55
New England Patriots, 17–23
New York Knicks, 9
NFL (National Football League)
    Arians's advocacy for Black
        coaches, 177
    Goodwin quote, 177
    number of Black players versus
        Black coaches, 177
    See also specific teams
Night School (film), 206
"no" as fortuitous, 31–41
    being malleable and, 36
    fine tuning an approach and, 40
    fixated on the closed door and,
        40–41
    pivoting as response, 31, 33–36
    searching for a "yes" and, 40
    Will and DJ job rejection, 33
    Will's film, *The Bottom,* 31–32
    working harder for a "yes," 34, 35,
        36–40
No Good Deed (film), 179

ABOUT THE AUTHOR

WILL PACKER, one of Hollywood's most influential and record-breaking filmmakers, has produced or executive produced a wide range of movies that together have grossed more than $1 billion worldwide at the box office, including ten films that opened at number one. He is a member of the esteemed Academy of Motion Picture Arts and Sciences and was selected as the producer of the 94th Academy Awards ceremony, for which he received an Emmy nomination. A longtime Atlanta resident, Packer is a limited partner of the Atlanta Falcons ownership group, serves on the board of the Atlanta Hawks Foundation, and is a longtime supporter of HBCU initiatives.

willpacker.com